Hooked on Cats

Hooked on Cats

Complete patterns and instructions for rug hookers

Joan Moshimer

Copyright © 1991 by Stackpole Books

Published by
STACKPOLE BOOKS
Cameron and Kelker Streets
P.O. Box 1831
Harrisburg, PA 17105

Printed in the United States of America

First Edition

10 9 8 7 6 5 4 3 2

Library of Congress Cataloging-in-Publication Data

Moshimer, Joan.
    Hooked on cats : complete patterns and instructions for rug hookers / Joan Moshimer. – 1st ed.
      p.   cm.
    Includes index.
    ISBN 0-8117-3041-7
    1. Hooking. 2. Cats in art. I. Title.
TT833.M67 1991
746.7′4 – dc20   90-47625
                                                             CIP

*To my granddaughters, Lily Deupree and
L.C. Moshimer, to my patient husband and
collaborator, Robert, and to my children
and their spouses, Paul, Pat, Jean, and Jesse,
ever supporting and cat lovers all*

Contents

Projects for Beginners

Intermediate and Advanced Projects

Acknowledgments

Thanks are owed to the many people who willingly shared with me their enthusiasm for both cats and rug hooking, not the least being Nora Pearse of Budleigh-Salterton, England, who first suggested that rug hooking and cats, so compatible, ought to be in a book together.

Many of my friends, with whom I have had spirited conversations about cats and hooked rugs, have helped to start me down exciting new avenues of exploration. To them I am sincerely grateful. I also give my thanks to Tammy Bernier, my patient and always helpful assistant who typed the manuscript (and who shares my love of hooking and cats). The generous antique dealers and others, who allowed us to photograph their rugs and show them on these pages are owed a debt of gratitude as well.

Thanks go to my editor Sally Atwater for her faith and wise counsel and to Mary Ellen Cooper of *Rug Hooking* magazine for her patience and encouragement.

My friend Susan Goldberg, who was always there with encouragement, support, and help, receives my thanks and love, as do the wonderful group of hookers who participated in the Hooked Cat Contest. Many of their rugs are proudly shown on these pages. It is obvious that their works bring together twin passions in their lives, the art of traditional rug hooking and their abiding love for the entire feline family.

Lastly, to all the cats who have shared my life – Kitty, Tom, Wilhelmina, Purry Como, Leo, Tinkerbell, Albert, Charlie, Goldie, and Momcat Mathilda – I say, "You taught me a lot about loyalty, patience, and forgiveness. I'll never forget you."

LEITH

Joan Leith Mortimer

Introduction

Do we really need another book about cats? Rug hookers do! This book brings cat lovers and rug hookers together. It was written for rug makers who love cats and for cat lovers who would like to learn how to hook. My friend Nora Pearse challenged me to write the book, and the more I thought about it, the more enthusiastic I became.

As the editor of a rug-hooking magazine for many years, I came into contact with thousands of ardent rug hookers. Seeing their talent and inventiveness led to the idea of holding a contest – a contest featuring hooked cats. We wondered whether there would be enough interest, since the area of competition was so specialized. But ruggers responded with enthusiasm, and the final number of entries exceeded 150. You can see many of the winning rugs, plus rugs that received honorable mentions, in the color section of this book.

My own experience with hooking cats has evolved through several styles. At first I hooked these wonderful creatures naturalistically, using my own pets for models. Then I found that "primitive" cats were loaded with charm, even though the style requires fewer colors and much less detail. It wasn't until I began to write this book that I discovered the fun of hooking "fancy cats," cats portrayed in unusual ways – with human faces or with their coats decorated with flowers. Inspired by the famed English artist, Louis Wain, we can hook cats that smile, smoke cigars, or wear monocles. A whole new world of hooking began to open up for me as I enjoyed these fanciful cats.

More than fifty million years ago, during the Eocene period, there appeared a short-legged, long-bodied little mammal that looked something like a weasel. This creature, called Miasis, was the ancestor of many of today's mammals, including bears, raccoons, dogs, hyenas, seals, sea lions, and cats.

I've tried to make this book helpful both to beginning rug hookers and to those who are old hands at hooking. For nonhooking cat lovers, there are easy-to-make cat projects and basic information on how to hook rugs. There is even a short glossary of rug-hooking terms. For those who are already rug makers, there are more advanced projects and tips on every aspect of hooking. How-to-dye instructions may be helpful and inspirational to both groups of readers.

Writing this book has been a labor of love and pleasure for me. I hope you will find it enjoyable and helpful.

Note: Since most rug hookers are female, a rug hooker is often referred to as "she." In this book, I have chosen to use "she" to avoid the cumbersome "he/she." I hope that the increasing number of men who are entering the craft will forgive the feminine pronoun.

Our Family of Cats

Wilhelmina was the matriarch of our family of seven cats. She was the undisputed boss and a very smart manager. She came to us in a roundabout way, although after she was contentedly installed with us, I had a distinct feeling that she had planned it all right from the beginning.

One Friday in autumn, my husband returned from a trip to our small company's headquarters in Dover-Foxcroft, a town in north central Maine almost at the edge of the wilderness. He told me that a small gray tiger cat was squeezing herself through a hole into the basement of the old building. She was obviously abandoned and looking for a warm place. The November nights were getting chilly, and soon the nights would be bitterly cold.

The people who worked in the office were kind to her and fed her, but she was in need of much more than that. The cellar where she spent her time was full of coal dust, so the little cat was filthy and unable to properly clean herself.

Since our previous cat had died, and we were feeling lonesome, we decided to bring the little gray tiger cat back to our home in Kennebunkport. She was afraid of me at first, but during the terrifying ride in a strange car, she soon accepted the comfort and reassurance of my lap and of my hands stroking her. From that time on, she was devoted to me.

The vet soon had her health problems solved, and it wasn't long before good food and loving attention made her sleek and gorgeous, confident of our affec-

The Encyclopedia of the Cat, by Angela Sayer, lists thirty-four kinds of cats in the world. Most people have probably never heard of the Chinese Desert Cat, the Black-Footed Cat of South Africa, the Flat-Headed Cat of Sumatra and Borneo, or the Kodkot of South America. The Iriomate Cat, which lives on a small island near Taiwan, was unknown until 1964. We may think we know something about domestic cats, those well-loved companions that share our lives, but how many of us could name the many, many varieties within the domestic cat family?

tion and certain that she was the queen of her new neighborhood.

We made a conscious decision to let her have one litter of kittens before having her spayed. At least, I made the decision and persuaded my husband to agree on the condition that I would find good homes for the little ones. As it turned out, I gave only one kitten away; the rest stayed with us!

"You found a good home for them all right," my husband declared bitterly, "right here!" But as time passed, he loved the cats as much as I did.

So there we were with Willie and her babies. The two sons, Leo and "Purry" Como, were classic gray tiger cats, almost identical in color and markings, male versions of their beautiful mother. Willie's daughter, Tinkerbell, was as dainty and flighty as the Peter Pan character for whom she was named.

Four was a nice number of pets to have, not too few and not too many. But fate stepped in again. Our son Paul asked me to take care of his pregnant cat Ishi while he was away on vacation. At the time, Willie's kittens were only about three weeks old, and the two adult females took an instant dislike to each other. Willie regarded Ishi as a threat to her premier position in the household, while poor Ishi, pregnant and among strangers, was highstrung and nervous. When her five kittens came earlier than expected, we were grateful that we had a house large enough to enable us to keep the two families reasonably apart. But it wasn't easy.

When Paul returned, he had found suitable homes for four of the five kittens. Since I had fallen in love with the entire cat family, I was only too happy to keep the last kitten. He was a chubby and lustrous brown tabby. We named him Fat Albert after Bill Cosby's childhood friend. If you looked straight down at him, his coloring appeared mostly black, but his sides revealed tawny lines of gray-browns and grays, blending together like a silken tapestry.

The first time Albert met Willie, he pounced playfully at her tail. I held my breath because even at the best of times, Willie had a short fuse, and she was still upset about the interlopers who had invaded her home. She gave Albert a strong cuff behind the ear that sent him dashing under the nearest chair. But for the rest of their life together he continued to dare to tease Willie, and she became fond of him in her own way. She would give him an occasional wash, something she denied her own two sons once they were beyond kittenhood. I think she admired his saucy ways with her.

One day when Albert had reached his adult growth, but while he was still green to the ways of the world, he came rushing in from outdoors with a large and beautiful woodcock held firmly in his jaws. He looked up at me as if to say, "What do I do with it now that I've caught it?" I knelt down and gently removed the bird from his mouth. The woodcock had no apparent injuries, so I took it outside to release it. It had gone into the frozen state that birds seem to instinctively adopt as a protective measure, and it lay in my hands for about five minutes. Then suddenly, to my great joy, it sprang into life and flew away. The culprit, Albert, seemed content with the way I solved his problem, and as far as we knew, he never caught another large bird.

Wilhelmina was very responsive when my husband started teaching her to sit on her haunches to take a small piece of hamburger from his fingers. The tricky part was to teach her to keep her forelegs hanging down at her sides without reaching up to grab at the morsel. She learned fast, and after her kittens had arrived and were growing up, they would imitate their mother. It was such fun to see them all lined up to receive their treats.

When the kittens were small, I worried about the fair amount of traffic that passes by our house. When the time came for the little cats to begin making exploratory trips outside, we decided to try to orient them away from the traffic and toward the back of the house where there was a large lawn and, beyond the fence, open fields bordered by thick woods. We

Throughout history, the mysterious and intelligent cat has swung from one extreme to another in the affections of mankind. At one end of the spectrum, the cat was cursed as a companion of evil witches; at the other, the cat was loved as the friend of the Virgin Mary. An early Christian story claims that at the moment of Jesus' birth in the stable, a kitten was born to a mother cat there.

opened a window in the laundry room just enough for the kittens to squeeze through. Then we propped a ladder outside under the window and wound 4-inch strips of rug wool around the uprights of the ladder. The kittens thought this was a wonderful arrangement, and it seemed to accomplish our purpose. All of the kittens except Fat Albert always headed for the fields and woods and stayed away from the traffic in front.

Albert liked to visit various friends across the street, but after some initial concern, we decided that he had become roadwise. He seemed to time his dashes across the street with great precision.

Willie's dainty little daughter Tinkerbell was her favorite. Every day for fourteen years, Tinkerbell would ask to be washed by her mother. When she came inside from a hunting trip, she would find Willie, wake her if she was napping, and stretch out her neck to be washed.

In Tinkerbell's early years, it was fairly common for her to take prolonged trips away from home. The first time that she was gone for a week, we made anxious trips to the local animal shelter looking for her. But after she had left several times, each time returning fit and full of life, we learned not to get too anxious about her. Her greatest pleasure upon returning home seemed to be the loving attention she unfailingly received from her mother.

Purry, who lived to the grand old age of eighteen, seemed to have been born purring. He was such a relaxed and calm creature that we naturally named him after Perry Como, the singer who epitomized an easygoing attitude. The name Purry Como served him well; he always began purring whenever anyone paid him the slightest attention. Occasionally, when Bob and I – and Purry – were relaxing during the evening, all it took to start him purring was for our eyes to meet!

Purry's brother Leo lived only two years. He had a kidney ailment and died in the animal hospital after an operation. We missed him greatly because he was a gentle giant of a cat without any meanness in him.

Shortly after Leo's passing, we became aware that the word had spread among the feline population of the town that our house put on an excellent free lunch for any cat daring to get past the resident cats. It wasn't long before we were adopted by Charlie, a huge old lion of a tomcat with several nicks missing from his ears, and Goldie, another large tom whose ginger coloring was a welcome relief from all of the grays. Charlie and Goldie had a certain amount of difficulty getting accepted by the resident cats, but both of the newcomers knew what they needed and stubbornly refused to be turned away. Eventually they achieved a state of grudging acceptance from the family, but it was conditional upon their acknowledging that Willie was mistress over all.

People have asked me if I used our cats as models for my hookings. The truth is, I used them all in one way or another. I often sketched them when they weren't looking. My main model was Purry. His portrait (albeit with somewhat different coloring) can be seen in the project "Tabby Cat."

Getting Started

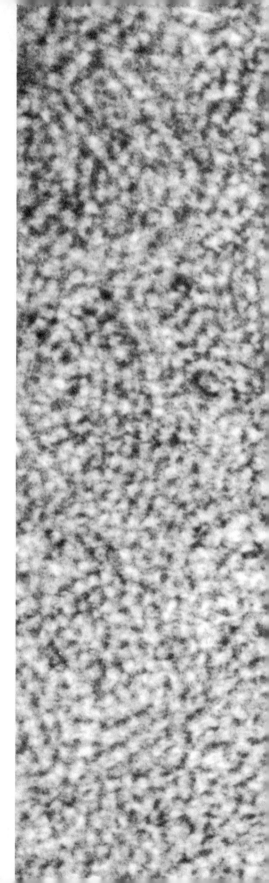

Basic Equipment

Rug hooking is one of the thriftiest crafts. Useful articles and beautiful decorative items are produced from the plainest and most prosaic of materials. Several of my hooking friends have commented, "Recycling is not new to us; we've been recycling old clothes for years!" It's true that rug hookers transform old clothes into floor coverings, wall hangings, and upholstery, as well as into handbags, hats, and clothing. They know that it *is* possible to make a silk purse out of a sow's ear!

In the last thirty years, the costs of hooking have risen sharply. You can spend a great deal of money on hundred-dollar frames, hand-dyed swatches, fancy cutting machines, and elaborate patterns. But the fact remains that anyone with a pair of scissors and two hands can cut strips from used wool clothing. Any sturdy fabric can serve as a backing; you can use burlap, linen, cotton, monk's cloth, or even a wool fabric that is open enough to be hooked into. A crochet hook can be adapted for rug hooking by a handy man or woman. And an old picture frame can serve admirably as a first frame. Ideas of *what* to hook abound. There is no reason not to begin this fascinating craft. If you get "hooked," then you can acquire more costly equipment.

I started hooking rugs in the 1950s, using a 75-cent hook and an old picture frame. I made a thick padding for the frame by winding 3-inch-wide strips of wool around its sides. Then I pinned my pattern to the

Cats have been at our hearths for at least 4,000 years. The ancient Egyptians regarded cats highly, employing them to guard their granaries against rats and mice. The Egyptians observed the way cats' eyes dilate and restrict like the waxing and waning of the moon; they worshipped the cat as the moon god Isis.

padding, using T-pins. There were lots of bare hardwood floors in our first home and only a small budget for rugs; there wasn't much money to buy equipment for my new passion, rug hooking. (The year that I started hooking rugs, my big Christmas present was a cutter.)

The basic pieces of equipment that you might want to buy are a frame and hooks. There are many rug-hooking frames available, usually from mail-order houses. (See Sources of Supplies.) They range from a simple frame like an embroidery hoop, either with or without a stand, to a picture-frame type. With the latter, the pattern is held either with ribbons of tiny wires or with thumbtacks.

Hooks vary in thickness. The fine hook, like a #8 crochet hook, is best for narrow (³⁄₃₂-inch) strips; the medium hook, like a #5 or #6 crochet hook, is useful for strips cut from ¹⁄₈ inch to ³⁄₁₆ inch wide; and the coarse hook, like a #3 crochet hook, is useful for wider strips. An extra-coarse hook, usually called a primitive hook, is preferred for very wide strips.

If you are a beginner, you should start with three sizes of hooks: fine, medium, and coarse. As you become acquainted with hooking and try different hooks, you will soon discover your own preferences. However, to begin with, use the medium hook and you won't go far wrong.

Here are two other suggestions for the novice rug hooker:

Start small. Select or design a small, uncomplicated pattern, and save the big, intricate hookings for subsequent projects, when you will have mastered the technique.

Make your first effort a hooked cat in the primitive or fancy-cat style, rather than a realistic, naturalistic portrayal. With primitives and fancy cats, you can use wools at hand and not have to custom-dye your fabrics. It's not that dyeing is difficult—on the contrary. And no-dye overdyeing is especially easy and very rewarding. But as beginners, we are all impatient and can hardly wait to behold our first finished piece. If you feel that anticipatory urge, by all means skip the chapters on dyeing and, once you've selected and prepared your fabrics, go right to the next step: cutting the strips and hooking them in.

Choosing Wools

Kinds of Wools

Remember "the man in the gray flannel suit"? Remember the suit and the wool flannel from which it was made? It was one hundred percent wool, soft and flexible, not too heavy and not too light. The wool in the gray flannel suit would have been ideal for rug hooking.

Much of the wool flannel we find today is only seventy or eighty percent wool; the rest of the fibers are man-made. Pure wool is the preferred material for rugs because of its strength, resilience, soil resistance, and color retention, but any wool blend that doesn't pull apart when it is cut into narrow strips may be used for making rugs. Wool of different weights may be used, too. The combination of weights and textures in a hooked piece gives textural interest, an attractive feature in hooking.

You can obtain new wool from mail-order houses (see Sources of Supplies), but don't overlook the value of cast-off clothing. Beautiful wool can often be found at thrift shops and yard sales, or you may receive wool clothing from friends and family who know you're looking for it. I'm told that even Sunbelt states can be rich sources of old wool clothing. New residents from cooler states bring their warm clothes when they move south and then discover that they don't need them. Rummage sales at retirement communities in the Sunbelt can be very rewarding.

Other Fabrics

Wool is ideal for rugs, but other hooked articles can be made of any fiber: cotton, rayon, velvet, chenille, silk, linen, even unusual materials, such as fur or grass. You can be especially adventurous in choosing materials when making a wall hanging. If you are in doubt about how any fabric will look when it is hooked, do a small test on a piece of burlap kept especially for that purpose. Pin or stitch a piece of the fabric next to the test hooking, and you will soon have a valuable reference guide for future use.

Treating Wools

If a fabric like a tweed seems to be too loosely woven to hold together for hooking, machine wash it in hot water (breaking all the rules for washing wools) to shrink it. Then dry it in a hot dryer to shrink it further. The idea is that the shrinking will pull the weave more tightly together, making it more likely to hold together when cut into strips.

If the weight of a wool seems just right, then of course you wouldn't take such drastic measures. But machine washing wool on a gentle cycle, using cold or warm water and a little detergent, won't hurt it. In fact, the washing action roughs up the smooth finish that characterizes much new wool, giving it a mellower look when hooked into a rug.

One of the best reasons for washing wool – especially used clothing – is to help protect it from moths. I have learned that moths are simply not interested in *clean* wool. It is only dirty wool that attracts them.

Once your used wool is clean and moth free, you can spend a relaxing time cutting and tearing the garments apart. Then you can dampen the wool again and iron the creases out or hang the pieces outside on a breezy day. Finally, roll the pieces up and tie them with a piece of the same wool for easy identification. You will come to regard a collection of wools, separated into color families, as a very real treasure.

Bastet was an Egyptian cat goddess worshipped about 30 B.C. She was considered the recipient of a higher vision and a symbol of man's noblest aspirations. A statue of Bastet is in the British Museum.

Useful Colors

Beginning hookers ask, "What color wool should I collect?" A good way to begin is to look for your favorite colors and to consider your favorite subjects. I assume, since you're reading this book, that one of your favorite subjects is cats, so you should save all the usual cat colors, such as creams, taupes, beiges, light and medium browns, gray-browns, pale grays, medium grays, dark grays, off-blacks, gold-beiges, gold-browns, rusty browns, dull oranges, rusts, taupy grays, and taupy browns. You may even think of a few more.

If you like to hook flowers and leaves into your rugs, then of course you would collect any lovely flower colors and greens. Greens are irresistible in their wondrous variety: light greens, medium greens, dark greens, yellow-greens, gray-greens, and blue-greens.

Or suppose you like blue, and one of your interests is collecting blue and white dishes and ornaments. You might like to hook something like the amusing "Staffordshire Cat" pattern for a doorstop or pillow. For this project, you would collect all the varieties of blue: light blues, medium blues, dark blues, green-blues, purple-blues, and every blue in between.

It is better to choose off-white wool or natural wool than pure white wool. White wool has been bleached in manufacturing, and occasionally some of the bleach remains, making the fabric difficult to dye. Also, white wool tends to visually jump out of a hooked piece, whereas off-white wool has a soft look.

Whatever your preferences, there are some colors in old wools that are always useful, especially for backgrounds. I'm thinking of lovely creamy beiges, oatmeals, and off-whites; soft celery greens; pale, grayed blue-greens; grayed dusty roses; and warm, mellow apricots. A seasoned rug hooker never passes up an opportunity to buy wools such as these, since she has learned from experience how useful they are.

Basic Dyeing

Of course, we all want beautifully colored wools for our rugs. Sometimes we can find useful mill-dyed swatches. Or we can obtain hand-dyed swatches from rug-hooking suppliers or teachers, but they are usually expensive.

Most rug hookers who are deeply committed to the craft learn to do custom dyeing themselves. They find that dyeing is a fascinating and fulfilling hobby that adds a totally new dimension to their hooking experience. If you have never tried dyeing wools, you are in for a happy surprise: dyeing is not difficult.

I taught myself to dye wools out of necessity. Hand-dyed swatches weren't available when I began to hook, and I had very little money to spend on wools, anyway. I kept a library book, *Rug Hooking and Braiding for Pleasure and Profit,* by Dorothy Lawless, at my elbow. Eventually I read every book that I could find on the subject; I attended dyeing demonstrations at Pearl McGown's workshops; and I studied with two fine teachers, Hallie Hall and the late Ruth Higgins. I found that I enjoyed dyeing. The beautiful colors that resulted from my efforts seemed to demand to be worked into hooking.

I used Cushing's Perfection dyes, which I obtained by mail from a small, hundred-year-old company located in Dover-Foxcroft, a little town in Maine. I had no way of knowing that before many years passed, my husband and I would accept an offer to buy that very company. That was in 1968. Today this little company supplies quality dyes not only to rug hookers, but also

*Our affectionate term **puss** may have been derived from **Pacht,** which was one of the names of Bastet. Another possibility is that **puss** is related to the Latin word **lepus,** which means **hare**, since in England **puss** was used to refer to both cats and hares.*

to housewives, art students, weavers, basketmakers, ballet companies, theaters, batikers, and many college and craft stores.

You will find the directions for dyeing wools easy to follow, and you will soon be admiring batches of wools in glorious colors that will help you make the rugs of your dreams. There is nothing like success to give a person confidence, and the wonderful thing about dyeing for rugs is that even the occasional "mistake" will eventually turn out to be useful, a blessing in disguise.

Directions for Basic Dyeing

Safety and Equipment. To dye successfully, you will need to acquire the necessary equipment and you will want to observe the safety precautions that good sense dictates. For example, you won't want to use your dye equipment for food preparation; use it exclusively for dyeing. When you are using dyes, put all foodstuff and dishes for food under cover. Be sure to work in a well-ventilated area or wear a protective face mask, and wear heavy rubber gloves, such as Playtex gloves, especially when dip-dyeing. When the dyeing is completed, wipe off all the countertops and the stove with damp paper towels.

If you cover a pan with aluminum foil, it is easy to get a steam burn when the foil is removed. Be careful to lift the edges of the foil gradually, even when wearing rubber gloves.

You will need the following equipment:

White enamel or stainless steel pans.

My favorite pan is 10 inches by 15 inches by 2 inches. Use a pan as close to that size as you can find. Department stores usually have a wide selection. You can also try restaurant supply stores (look in the Yellow Pages). And don't neglect yard sales and flea markets. I have gradually built up a supply of pans and lids in different sizes, so I always have what I need.

A long barbeque fork, preferably stainless steel.
A set of measuring spoons, including a dye-measuring spoon.

> A dye-measuring spoon, available from hooking suppliers or teachers, measures ¼ teaspoon on the large end and ¹/₃₂ teaspoon on the small end.

Glass measuring cups, 1-cup, 2-cup, and 4-cup, two each.
A pair of tongs.
Several stainless steel spoons for stirring.
A selection of Cushing's Perfection dyes.

> Tan and Silver Gray for gray tiger cats; Black, Dark Brown, and Navy Blue for black cats; Taupe, Silver Gray, and Dark Gray for slate-gray cats; Ecru and Champagne for tan-gold cats, bobcats, and mountain lions; Golden Brown and Rust for ginger cats; Orange and Maize for calico cats and tigers; Old Ivory, Dark Brown, and Khaki Drab for Siamese cats.

White paper towels.
Uniodized salt.
White vinegar.
Bleach for cleaning dye stains from pans.
Aluminum foil to cover pans without lids.

Equivalents and Abbreviations

Equivalents
    3 teaspoons = 1 tablespoon
    16 tablespoons = 1 cup

    For use with a dye-measuring spoon:
    large end = ¼ teaspoon
        2 dips of large end = ½ teaspoon
        3 dips of large end = ¾ teaspoon
        4 dips of large end = 1 teaspoon
    small end = ¹/₃₂ teaspoon
        2 dips of small end = ¹/₁₆ teaspoon
        4 dips of small end = ⅛ teaspoon
Abbreviations
    t. = teaspoon
    T. = tablespoon

Preparing the Wool for Dyeing. Presoak the wool that you intend to dye in a mixture of warm water and a little dishwashing detergent, such as Ivory Liquid. (Sometimes rug hookers refer to this solution as Ivory water.)

When the wool is wet, it will appear considerably darker than dry wool. If you are trying to dye the wool to match another piece, you will also need to wet the original piece for comparison. Remember, too, that if you are dyeing over colored wool, the original color will affect the outcome. (See Overdyeing for Beauty.)

Mixing the Dye Solution. To prepare the dye solution, you usually measure about ½ teaspoon of the dry dye into a measuring cup and add 1 cup of boiling water. Stir for about a minute to thoroughly dissolve the dye.

Those amounts can differ considerably, however, depending on the formula being used and the dye job to be done. The amount of dye to be used also depends on the strength of the particular dye. On the Cushing's dye color card, some of the colors shown are pale and weak, some are of medium strength, and others are dark and intense. The color value shown is what we can expect when one package of that dye is dyed over one pound of wool. Therefore, the color card tells us that some dyes are stronger than others and that we may need to use different amounts of different dyes.

It is convenient to keep a small, screw-top jar partly filled with uniodized salt in your work area. You can clean your dye-measuring spoon by rubbing it in the salt. And when the salt eventually becomes colored, after many dyeing jobs, you can find a good use for it. Sprinkle the colored salt on several layers of wet wool of any darkish color. Layer the wool in a pan, pour a little water at the side of the pan to avoid disturbing the dye, cover the pan, and bake the wool at 300 degrees F. for about an hour or until the water is clear. (You may need to add more water during the baking time.) You will find many interesting uses for these wools, such as outlining, defining leaf veins, and making shadows in pictorials. The resulting colors may be grayed blues, grayed greens, grayed reds, grayed golds, and so on. These wools are sometimes referred to as mud, since they tend to be dull and uninteresting, at least to people who don't hook. But rug hookers find them perfect for a variety of uses.

Preparing the Dye Bath. Put enough hot tap water into an enamel pan to comfortably cover the wool when it is added, and put the pan over medium heat. Immediately add about 1 tablespoon of the dye solution. Then add the unrinsed wool, stirring well with a long fork.

As the dye bath nears the boiling point, the dye migrates more quickly into the wool, causing a certain amount of uneven dyeing. The more you stir the dye bath as it approaches the boiling point or when it is boiling, the more even the dyeing will be. However, uneven dyeing is often considered desirable for rug hooking, especially in backgrounds.

If you add too much dye to the dye bath, your wool may become too dark, and it is difficult to lighten it. It is smart to add only a small amount of dye at the beginning. Then, after the wool has simmered in the dye bath for a few minutes, you can check the color. If the color is not dark enough, remove the pan from the heat, add a small amount of dye, stirring vigorously as you do, and put the pan back on the heat. When the dye bath has returned to a simmer, again, give the wool enough time to absorb the dye before checking the color again.

When the desired color is achieved, add about 1 tablespoon of salt for every quart of water in the dye bath. Cover the pan and simmer for 30 minutes to set the color. (Simmer for 45 minutes for dark colors.)

Rinsing the Wool. Always rinse the dyed wool at least three times. I usually rinse once by hand and then let the wool go through an entire cycle in the washing machine without detergent. That way, the wool is rinsed twice in the machine. (Some people prefer to wash the newly dyed wool with detergent before rinsing it, but I'm not convinced that washing is necessary.)

Dip-Dyeing

In dip-dyeing, the range of values from dark to light is dyed right into your strip. Dip-dyeing is a favorite of mine because it is easy to do and produces little waste.

When a dip-dyed strip is hooked in, the shading is automatic. If the strip doesn't change value quickly enough to suit you, then you can pull the loop higher and snip the excess off. Save those pieces! They may be just what you need in another area. For easy selection, I keep them in neat little piles of light, medium, and dark values.

You can cut some wools with either the warp or the weft and get satisfactory results. Others are not so versatile; strips cut with the weft pull apart as they are hooked even though strips cut with the warp don't. When dip-dyeing, use pieces of wool that can be cut either way. You will then be able to get strips of a single color or strips that have varying values (strips shading from light to dark or making a smooth transition from one color to another). There are many times when having this choice will be useful.

Of course, if you use a narrow piece of wool, you will be able to cut only one way. It is best to use a large piece of wool; the dimensions of the wool should match the size of a flat pan that is 10 inches by 15 inches. In dip-dyeing, the wool piece is usually held by the narrower end, so that the values run light to dark along the length of the fabric.

To dip-dye with Taupe (a good cat color), put ½ teaspoon of the dye into 1 cup of boiling water, and stir well. If you dye three pieces of wool, I suggest that you use one piece that is off-white, one that is tan, and one that is pale gray.

Presoak the wool pieces for a few minutes in warm Ivory water.

To prepare the dye bath, use a 2- or 3-quart white

enamel saucepan. Add hot tap water to a depth of 3 or 4 inches, 1 tablespoon of white vinegar, and 1 tablespoon of the dye solution. Bring the dye bath to a boil, and keep it boiling over high heat. As the dipping is done, the dye bath will reduce to a simmer.

Wearing rubber gloves, hold a piece of wet wool by the narrow end and dip the other end into the dye bath to a depth of about 3 inches. Don't hold it still or a line will form; keep moving it slightly up and down, giving the end of the wool a chance to absorb some dye. This will be the darker end. As you continue to dip the wool, go deeper and deeper into the weakening dye bath. At this point, you will get medium and medium-light values. Be patient; this process takes a little time. After a few minutes, as the dye is transferred to the wool, the dye bath will begin to get very weak. This is when you will get the lightest values at the top end.

If the dye bath becomes too weak, you can add a small amount of dye solution and then redip the wool, concentrating on getting light values at the end. The dye bath will probably not clear entirely, so it is best to prepare a fresh dye bath before changing colors.

To set the dye after the dipping is completed, lay the dyed wool flat in the enamel pan. You can set as many as eight pieces at a time. Lay one piece of wool on top of another with the darkest pieces at the bottom; layer the pieces with a dark end on a dark end and a light end on a light end. If there is a difference in color value between two pieces of wool, separate them with white paper towels and put the lightest pieces on top. If the difference between a light piece of wool and a dark piece is really dramatic, set them separately.

Sprinkle a tablespoon or more of salt on each layer of wool. Then add ¼ cup of vinegar to 1½ cups of hot water, and pour enough of this mixture over the wools to thoroughly moisten them. Cover the wools in the pan and bake them at 325 degrees F. for 30 minutes and then at 300 degrees F. for 1 hour, or until the water is clear. Don't allow the wools to become dry; add

*The term **tabby** probably comes from an area inside the city of Baghdad called Attabiya, where a watered taffeta was once produced. The random design on the taffeta was similar to the markings on some of the local cats, which came to be known as **tabby** cats.*

more hot water during the baking time if necessary. Rinse the wools carefully and allow them to dry.

Spot-Dyeing

Spot-dyeing is a method that, like dip-dyeing, produces surprising and lovely blends of color that will add a lot to the quality of your work. Unlike dip-dyeing, however, the pretty spots of color on a spot-dyed piece change value in unpredictable ways. Therefore, when hooking with spot-dyed wools, cut pieces only as you need them. Making your selections from the uncut wool allows you to use the beautiful patterns of color to their best advantage.

The formulas I've suggested give dull blacks, brownish rusts, pale rusts, and creamy whites – colors that are very desirable for hooking cats. If you prefer a brighter orange tone to the brownish rusts, substitute orange dye for the apricot.

For wool, you'll need two pieces of light gray, two pieces of light yellow, two pieces of off-white, and two pieces of gray or brown tweed. The pieces should be the same size as your pan, usually 10 inches by 15 inches.

For spot-dyeing, you do not make a dye bath, as you did for basic dyeing and dip-dyeing. Instead, prepare the dye solutions by mixing a small amount of dye with boiling water in a measuring cup.

Dye Solutions
A = 1/8 t. Apricot and 1/32 t. Silver Gray in 1 cup boiling water
B = 1/16 t. Black in 1/2 cup boiling water

After presoaking in Ivory water, take one piece of light gray wool and lay it in the pan. Add a mixture of 1 cup hot water and 1 tablespoon white vinegar to the pan and put it over moderate heat.

Now apply 2 tablespoons of A to the upper left corner. Rub the dye over the wool with back of a spoon as shown.

Next, apply 4 teaspoons of *B* to the same corner as shown.

Put the second piece of light gray on top of the first and apply the dyes in exactly the same way.

A piece of yellow wool goes on next. Apply 1 tablespoon of *A* to the upper left corner. Then apply 2 teaspoons of *B* to the corner, and rub as before. Sprinkle 2 tablespoons of uniodized salt over the wool.

The second yellow piece goes on over the first and is dyed in the same way.

Next dye a piece of off-white wool using 1 tablespoon of *A* and 2 teaspoons of *B*. Then add the last piece of white wool but do not apply any dye.

Wearing gloves, gently push the wool down to absorb some of the dye from the other pieces. Sprinkle 2 tablespoons of salt over the wool. Then add a mixture of 1 tablespoon of white vinegar and two cups of boiling water to the pan.

Cover the pan tightly with foil and let it simmer for 45 minutes. Add more water if necessary.

If you prefer, you can put the pan in at 350° for 15 minutes, then lower the temperature to 300° and leave it in for 45 minutes more. Rinse well and dry.

Now, with the rest of the dyes and the two pieces of gray or brown tweed, you can dye some useful dark values. Use 10-inch by 15-inch pieces. If you're lucky enough to have some odd-sized tweed pieces that add up to approximately the same size, use them.

Presoak the pieces in Ivory water, then loosely arrange them in the bottom of a dye pan (the 1½-quart size will do). Simply pour the rest of *A* on the left side and the rest of *B* on the right side. Add 2 tablespoons of salt and turn on the heat. Allow to simmer for 5 minutes, then add 2 cups of boiling water and simmer, covered, for another 25 minutes. Rinse well and dry.

Dyeing Yarn

Dyeing yarn is really not very different from dyeing wool. Yarn can be dip dyed or spot dyed, as well as dyed a single color. The only difference is in the way

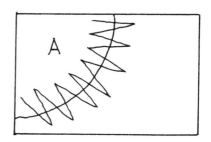

Above: *The zigzag lines show where to rub the wool with the back of a spoon. This blends the dyes and helps the wool absorb them.* **Below:** *B is applied over A and rubbed in the same way.*

To prepare yarn for dyeing, tie the skein loosely in several places using plain white string. Now the yarn can be dyed and rinsed without becoming tangled.

we prepare the yarn for dyeing. Yarn is dyed in a skein, and you must be careful to keep it from tangling during the dyeing and rinsing process.

Lay the skein of yarn in an oval shape on a table. Then tie plain white string loosely around it in about ten places. The strings must be securely tied, but they must be loose enough to give the yarns access to the dye in the dye bath.

Presoak the skein just as you would presoak wool, and then dye the yarn, following the directions for dyeing wool fabric.

Overdyeing for Beauty

Every scrap of wool cloth, no matter how awful or how brilliant the colors, can be made usable by overdyeing, that is, dyeing *over* the original color. Of course, the original color will have an effect on the final result. I cannot think of a better way to learn about color – to see how one color affects another – than by overdyeing. There is a thrill of discovery when an ugly-duckling purple turns out to be a rich plum, or when a bright Kelly green mellows into a soft olive.

You will find the guidelines in this chapter helpful as you begin to experiment with overdyeing. Remember that the darker the original color, the stronger the dye bath should be. If the original color is pale, the dye bath can be weaker.

You can combine several different wools in the same dye bath if you are planning to use them for a background. The original colors must be similar, such as several shades of green. When you remove the wools from the dye bath, they will still be various shades, but they will be more closely related, having been unified by the overdyeing. When the overdyed pieces are hooked in, they will produce an attractive marbleized effect.

If you overdye a wool that has a rather loose weave, immersion in the dye bath will shrink it and actually make it more suitable for hooking.

Directions for Overdyeing

To make the dye solution, measure about ¼ teaspoon of dye into a measuring cup. (You can add up to one teaspoon of dye for darker values.) Add one cup of boiling water to the cup and stir thoroughly.

If you are new to dyeing, I suggest that you work with only half a yard of wool at a time, about the equivalent of a woman's skirt, ripped apart. Choose a stainless steel or white enamel pan that is big enough to comfortably hold the wool. I prefer to use a white enamel pan, because the white interior helps me judge the colors.

Presoak the wool for a few minutes in warm water with a tablespoon of dishwashing liquid, such as Ivory, added to it. (This helps the wool take the dye.) After presoaking the wool, put it directly into the pan, without rinsing out the detergent, and cover it with hot water. Add a teaspoon or two of the dye solution and stir it well. Then put the pan over heat and bring the water to a boil, stirring occasionally. When the water is boiling or nearly boiling, add a tablespoon or two of salt or vinegar. At this point, the dye will be quickly taken up by the wool. If you turn off the heat while you are adding the salt or vinegar, the dye will go into the wool more evenly. Then you can turn on the heat again and continue to simmer the solution. You may want to add more dye solution, depending on how dark the wool is and how dark you want it to be.

It may be difficult to judge the color of the wool if it is a dark color; wools are always a shade darker when wet, but dark colors look almost black when they are in the dye bath. Remove a small piece of wool, press the excess water out of it with a towel, and then examine it in a good light. When you are satisfied with the color, allow the solution to simmer for 30 minutes for light colors or up to 60 minutes for dark colors.

When the wool is removed from the dye bath, it must be thoroughly rinsed in at least three rinse waters to remove the salt or vinegar. I always rinse it once by hand and twice in the washing machine, using the rinse cycle and without adding detergent. Some rug hookers wash the freshly dyed wools before rinsing them. When the wool has been rinsed, it can be dried naturally or in the dryer at a warm setting.

Besides being beautiful, the markings on a tabby cat serve to camouflage the animal when it hunts. In dappled shade beneath a canopy of sunlit leaves or in long grasses, the markings on a tabby cat break up its outline and make it difficult to see.

It is unlikely that your wool pieces will be evenly dyed; in fact, they will probably be slightly uneven, but this is exactly the effect you need. When you cut the wool into strips and hook them in, your hooking will be more beautiful because of the subtle variation in shades.

I heartily recommend that you keep a notebook on dyeing. Paste samples of wool in the notebook to show the colors before and after dyeing; note the color and quantity of dye that you used; and record the amount of wool that was dyed (weigh it if you can't measure it). These notes will be a valuable reference, well worth the extra effort.

Guidelines for Overdyeing

Dyeing over Yellow Wool

green dye gives	yellow-green
blue dye gives	green
purple dye gives	gray
red dye gives	orange
brown dye gives	golden brown

Dyeing over Orange Wool

yellow dye gives	golden yellow
green dye gives	grayed brown
blue dye gives	gray*
purple dye gives	brown
red dye gives	tangerine

Dyeing over Green Wool

blue dye gives	aqua
purple dye gives	grayed brown
red dye gives	gray*
brown dye gives	olive green
yellow dye gives	yellow-green

*Off-black will result from a strong dye over dark shades of wool.

——————— *Dyeing over Brown Wool* ———————

yellow dye gives	golden brown
green dye gives	olive green
blue dye gives	gray*
purple dye gives	purplish brown
red dye gives	red-brown

——————— *Dyeing over Turquoise or Aqua Wool* ———————

blue dye gives	green-blue
purple dye gives	grayed blue
red dye gives	grayed red or grayed blue-green*
brown dye gives	grayed brown
yellow dye gives	green

——————— *Dyeing over Blue Wool* ———————

red dye gives	purple
brown dye gives	grayed brown or grayed blue*
yellow dye gives	green
purple dye gives	plum
green dye gives	aqua

——————— *Dyeing over Purple Wool* ———————

red dye gives	wine
brown dye gives	off-black
yellow dye gives	gray
green dye gives	grayed brown
blue dye gives	plum

——————— *Dyeing over Red, Rose, and Pink Wool* ———————

brown dye gives	dull orange-red
yellow dye gives	orange
green dye gives	gray*
blue dye gives	purple
purple dye gives	wine

*Off-black will result from a strong dye over dark shades of wool.

No-Dye Overdyeing

No-dye overdyeing is a way to "marry" colors without using actual dye. Remember, there is dye present in colored wools, and rug hookers can make use of that dye.

When variously colored wools are presoaked for a few minutes in warm water and dishwashing liquid, and then simmered for a while, their colors are released. For example, when yellows are simmered in the same pan with blues, the yellow color that is released will enter the blue wools, and the blue color that is released will enter the yellow wools. The result is a group of slightly varying greens.

Since there is such a variety of colors in wools, and since some colors bleed more than others, the results can be surprising. But we can make a few generalizations. For example, reds usually bleed a lot, so they should be used in relatively small amounts with other wools, or the red will overwhelm any other color. Putting two complementary-colored wools (red and green, blue and orange, or yellow and purple) in the same pot will yield softened, grayed colors. Simmering several shades of the same color together will give a treasury of colors that are different from each other and yet friendly with each other, too. This is the marrying process.

Try simmering together a variety of pale greens for a beautiful background of leaves and grass; a group of light and medium blues for a great sky; some yellows, creams, and small amounts of purple-reds for fruits and flowers; and golds, tans, taupes, grays, and light-to-medium browns for earth and rocks.

The method of no-dye overdyeing is simple. In a pot of water, place the presoaked colored wools that you want to mix. Simmer the wools for about 30 minutes. Then add a few tablespoons of salt and simmer for another 15 minutes. Remove the wool pieces, rinse them thoroughly, and dry them. As you can see, this method is another inexpensive way to obtain beautiful wools for our craft.

Onion-Skin Dyeing

Onion-skin dyeing, like no-dye overdyeing, is a way to move colors that are already present in the wool from one piece to another. This method takes advantage of the color that is present in onion skins. The skins also cause colors to blend and soften and take on an indefinable glow.

First Method.   For this procedure you will need your large pan, dish-washing liquid, uniodized salt, the dry outer skins of yellow onions, and about a dozen pieces of wools in various colors.

When selecting wools for onion-skin dyeing, remember that some colors, such as red, royal blue, and Kelly green, bleed more than others. When using these colors, use small amounts. You can use new or old wools and whatever colors you like, including tweeds and checks. It's best to have a range of darks, mediums, and lights. As for size, use pieces of wool that will fit in your pan without crowding.

Soak the woolens for a few minutes in hot water mixed with 3 tablespoons of dishwashing liquid to help the wool absorb colors. Next, without rinsing out the detergent, lightly squeeze the water from the darkest piece and lay it in the bottom of the pan. Just drop it in; it doesn't have to lie flat.

Now, take a handful of onion skins and scatter them over the wool. Sprinkle about a tablespoon of salt over the skins and the wool.

Lightly wring out the next darkest piece and place it over the first piece. Add another handful of skins and another tablespoon of salt. Progressing from the darkest pieces through the mediums and finishing with lights, continue alternating layers of wool with skins and salt until all the wool is in the pan.

Pour hot or boiling water over the layers until everything is covered. Bring the stew to a boil, cover, and simmer without stirring for 30 to 45 minutes. Finally, rinse thoroughly three times as you do whenever you dye.

Second Method.   This technique for onion-skin dyeing is very similar to the first, but it isn't quite so messy. Rather than adding the onion skins directly to the pan with the wool, you prepare a dye bath from the skins.

Fill an old nylon stocking with dried onion skins. Then put the stocking into a large pan of hot water and bring to a simmer. You'll see the color pour out of the skins, making a richly colored dye bath.

In another large pan, arrange the pieces of wool as before, dark to light. Add salt between each layer but not onion skins.

Now, remove the stocking from the first pan and discard. Pour the colored water over the wool in the second pan and simmer it as outlined above.

If you use this second method and are dyeing only lights and mediums, dilute the onion water with plain water so that the color isn't overwhelming. You'll learn quickly how to adjust the strength of the onion water to the color of the wools.

Cutting the Strips

Cutting with the Warp or Weft

After you have collected, cleaned, and dyed your wools, it is time to cut them into strips. There are long threads in wool, the *warp* threads that run the full length of the fabric, parallel to the selvage, and the *weft* threads that run across the fabric from selvage to selvage. In many fabrics, you can cut strips either with the warp or with the weft. Sometimes a wool that has been washed and dried has developed a fuzz, so that it can be successfully cut either way. But with some fabrics, strips cut parallel to the weft will not hold together. In most cases, the best way to cut strips is parallel to the selvage.

If you find that a check or tweed can be cut either with the warp or with the weft of the fabric, take some time to study how the strips will look. Sometimes strips cut across the fabric are slightly different from those cut down the fabric; they may appear darker or lighter and they may produce different looks when hooked in.

The Length and Width of Strips

You can work with strips as short as 2 or 3 inches. And when working fairly large areas of background, you may use quite long strips, up to 36 inches. But the usual length of strips, the length that is easiest to work with, is 12 inches.

The width of the strips can vary from a little less

The strip on the left has been cut with the warp. The long threads hold the strip together. The strip on the right, however, has been cut on the bias and has nothing to hold it together.

There is certain evidence that cats were in England during the Roman Empire: to this day, their paw prints can be seen on tiles excavated from Roman towns.

than ⅛ inch to a little more than ¼ inch. When the strips are pulled through the backing, their height is usually about the same as the width of the strip used. Strips that are ⅛ inch wide are usually pulled about ⅛ inch high; and strips that are ¼ inch wide usually produce ¼-inch loops. This just happens without the rug hooker's giving it any thought.

Of course, if you consciously work at it, you can make the loops an inch high if you want, but usually you can expect to have a thicker rug using strips ¼ inch wide and a thinner rug using narrower strips. This is an interesting point that surprises rug hookers who haven't considered it before. When the strips are wider, we tend to pull the loops higher and the rug is thicker. When the strips are narrow, we pull the loops less high and the rug is thinner.

Formerly, wide strips were used mostly by enthusiasts of primitive-style hookings. But today it is becoming more common to see wide strips worked into glorious rugs and wall hangings of other styles as well. A real advantage to using wide strips is that the work progresses much faster. For those of us who work outside our homes, the little time we have for relaxation must be well spent. Wide strips enable us to complete a project more quickly; this is an important consideration, especially when you're making a large rug. The only disadvantage to using wide strips is that a rug will take more wool, but to many of us, the pleasure of a thicker, more luxurious rug is worth it.

If you are hooking a small table mat or chair pad, you might prefer to use a narrower strip to produce a thinner, more detailed piece. Some rug hookers prefer to use narrow strips even for large rugs. The rugs can be very beautiful with great detail and with literally hundreds of colors and values in them. But a large rug may take several years to make. Before beginning such a project, we need to ask ourselves, "Do I have the time, energy, and dedication to complete this rug?" Your answer will depend on your own temperament and circumstances.

In some hooked pieces, we are using so many different textures and weights of wools that we may combine several widths of strips out of necessity. To pull strips through the backing with ease, a thick wool needs to be cut into narrower strips and a thin wool needs to be cut into wider strips.

As you gain experience in rug hooking, you will see the factors that influence your choice of how wide to cut the strips of wool: the desired thickness of the finished piece, the style of the piece, the amount of wool available, the thickness of the wool, and the amount of time you want to spend on a project.

The Amount of Wool Needed

Once you have decided how wide you want to cut the strips, you can address the question, "How much wool will I need for this project?" Remember that if you use wider strips, you will need more wool.

A general rule of thumb is that for a rug using ⅛-inch strips, you can multiply the area of the rug by five to find out the amount of wool needed to make the rug. In other words, five layers of 2- by 3-foot wool should be plenty to hook a 2- by 3-foot rug.

Another way to figure how much wool you will need for a specific project is to hook a small sample piece, using strips of the width you have chosen for the project. Hook a small square area, about 4 inches by 4 inches, and keep track of the amount of wool you use. You can weigh the finished test piece, subtracting the weight of the backing, to measure the wool that was used. Using your sample as a guide, you can more accurately estimate the amount of wool you will need for the complete project. Always add a bit more for good measure.

Cutting the Strips

I would suggest that new rug hookers cut strips about ³⁄₁₆ inch wide. This is an easy width to cut by hand, and if you cut the strips a little narrower or wider in places, it won't hurt. The main thing to re-

The cutter, a hand-cranked machine that can cut several even strips at a time, is a godsend to busy rug hookers.

Cutter Head Widths

Cut	Width of Strips
#3	3/32 inch
#4	4/32 (1/8)
#5	5/32
#6	6/32 (3/16)
#7	7/32
#8	8/32 (1/4)

member is to cut the strips on the straight of the fabric, using a torn edge as a guide. If your wool is a tweed or something that resists being torn, cut a long, straight edge by following a single thread. Work with a piece of wool about 4 inches wide, so that you can easily see if you begin to cut crookedly.

Most rug hookers eventually invest in a cutter. There are cutting machines available that cut up to five strips at a time easily and evenly. They certainly speed up the process of cutting, leaving more of our valuable time for hooking. Note that cutting machines work best with wool; they may not be as satisfactory with other fabrics.

Designs and Patterns

Creating a Design

If you buy a design that is prestamped on burlap or other backing, you are ready to begin hooking immediately. But you may want to create your own design, to express your individual vision and originality.

An interesting way to create a design is to use a favorite slide of your cat or cats. Tape your backing to the wall in place of the screen, and project the image of your slide onto it. You can adjust the size by moving the projector closer to the screen or farther away from it.

Then it is an easy matter to draw the outline of your design directly onto the backing with a felt-tip pen. If you want to make a more detailed design, project and copy the image on white paper instead of on the backing. Then you can add design details before transferring the pattern to your backing.

Another way to create your own design is to cut out the dominant figures, say a cat and her kittens, and place them on a large piece of paper that has the dimensions of the finished rug. Move the cut-outs on the paper until you have an arrangement that pleases you. Then draw around each cutout figure to create your pattern.

Some rug hookers can draw a full-size design directly on the backing, but for most of us, it is easier to first work out the design in a small sketch. See "Specific to Cats" for help with designing a pattern that features cats.

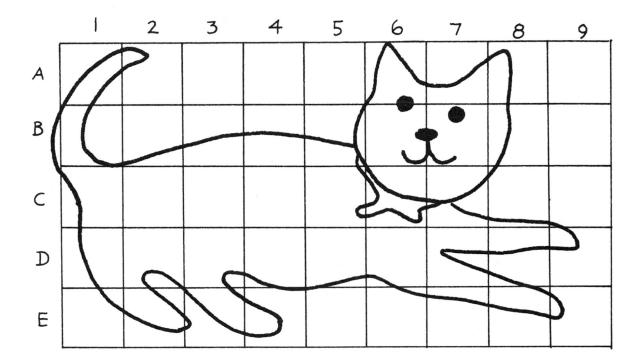

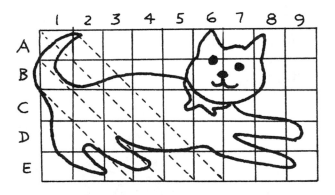

The original sketch is done on a small grid. Letters and numbers identify each square. Enlarge the design by making a bigger grid of the same number of squares. Then the details of each square on the small grid are transcribed onto the corresponding square of the large grid. For especially complicated designs you may want to draw diagonal lines through the squares to give you more reference points.

Enlarging the Design

It is usually best to make your original design small. The proportion and balance, or lack of proportion and balance, show up more readily on a small sketch. Of course, before transferring the design to your backing, you must enlarge the design to the size of the finished rug.

Begin by dividing your design into squares. You can trace your design onto Quickdraft tracing vellum by Dietzgen or a similar product. Quickdraft has ¼-inch grids printed on it. The squares can be any size, although the more detailed your design is, the smaller the squares should be. If you have an extremely detailed design, you may want to draw diagonal lines in addition to the squares.

You will need a piece of paper large enough to accommodate the enlarged design; the paper will be as large as the finished rug. You can use good quality tracing paper, white newsprint, or lightweight brown paper. Draw your rectangle or square or circle or oval, depending on the shape of your rug, with the dimensions you want the finished rug to be. A large T-square is useful for keeping the 90-degree angles correct and for ruling long, straight lines. In a pinch, you can check your angles with any square corner, and an ordinary yardstick can serve as a straightedge.

Then divide the rectangle, square, circle, or oval that represents your finished rug into the same number of squares on which you worked out your small design. This is a matter of simple arithmetic. If there were nine squares across the top of your small design, and if your finished rug is to be 36 inches wide, you would divide 36 by 9. The enlarged squares would then each be 4 inches on a side. If there were five squares down the side of your original design, then there would be five 4-inch squares down the side of the enlarged design, making it 20 inches long. Use a ballpoint pen to draw the squares for the enlarged design.

To create the enlarged design, study the original

design square by square. In each square of the enlarged design, carefully draw what you see in each corresponding square of the original design. Use a pencil to draw the design. You will be surprised at how easy it is to draw the enlarged design using the squares as your guidelines.

Transferring the Design

If you are working with a simple geometric design, such as the "Four Kittens" project presented in this book, in which the motifs are enclosed in regularly spaced squares or other geometric shapes, you may be able to draw the design directly onto your backing. Even if you are sure you can't draw a straight line, you will find that you can. If you pull a sharp pencil between two threads of the backing material, you will quickly see just how easy it is to draw a perfectly straight line. This ability is a valuable one to a budding rug designer.

Another method for transferring uncomplicated designs is to trace the design onto bridal tulle, the thin, open fabric used for bridal veils. First go over your enlarged design with a thick, black felt-tip pen (Sharpie is a good brand for this purpose). Then place a piece of tulle over your design and trace the design onto the tulle, using a thin, black felt-tip pen. Place the tulle over the backing and tape it securely, so that it doesn't move when you work. As you go over the lines of the design with the thick felt-tip pen, the ink from the pen will penetrate the thin tulle and mark the backing.

One more method for transferring simple designs is to trace the design onto good-quality tracing paper. Then turn the paper over and go over the lines with a dark crayon, working on the back of the paper. Place the paper over the backing with the crayoned side against the backing. Secure the paper at the top with tape; don't tape the bottom edge, because you will need to lift it to see whether the pattern is transferring correctly. Press the pattern on the backing with a hot

Cats have often been valued for their help in keeping the rat and mouse population down. In the tenth century, the Welsh King Howel the Good created a system for grading cats and establishing their value. The price of a young kitten was one penny; the price of an older kitten that had caught a mouse was twopence; and the price of a healthy cat, which had proved it was a good hunter, was fourpence.

iron until the crayon lines transfer to the backing. (Don't iron over the tape.) If your design is too large to be conveniently placed on an ironing board, make an ironing pad of a thick layer of newspapers covered with a folded cotton sheet on the floor.

To transfer more detailed designs, use an iron-on pattern pencil, available from craft and rug-hooking supply stores and from mail-order houses. The iron-on pattern pencil works similarly to the crayon method. After tracing the design onto tracing paper, turn the paper over and trace the lines on the reverse side with the pattern pencil, making strong, dark lines.

Place the pattern over the backing with the penciled side against the backing. With the pattern and backing on an ironing board or ironing pad, press it with an iron set for cotton. Be sure the pattern doesn't move while you are ironing. If you are ironing on a homemade pad, anchor the pattern with large cans of soup or something similar. Run the iron slowly over the design; be patient, allowing enough time for the lile to be transferred. The line will turn blue as it transfers. You can lift a corner of the pattern, being careful not to displace it, to check your progress. When all the lines show clearly on the backing, the pattern has been transferred.

In an attempt to speed up the process, some rug hookers like to place a sheet of aluminum foil beneath the rug backing with the shiny side up to reflect the heat. Try it if you like.

Backgrounds

Many beginning rug hookers, and even some experienced ones, have been heard to say as they are hooking the design on their rugs, "I haven't decided what color to use in the background yet." This is a big mistake!

Backgrounds are an important element in hooked rugs. There is a very real relationship between the design elements and the spaces behind them. The background must be considered at the beginning of the design process, so that it will be compatible with the design. When there is a unity between the background and the design, it enhances the entire rug.

Even the word *background* implies that it is unimportant. But think of the interior walls of our homes. They provide the background for all of our carefully chosen furniture, window coverings, and accessories. They are far from unimportant. In fact, how to treat the walls is one of the first decisions we make regarding an undecorated room. We consider whether the walls should be plain, faintly patterned with a subtle wallpaper, or treated boldly with a large design that will be a dominant part of the room's decor.

Translating our care in choosing the background for a room into considerations about the background of a rug we are planning, we ask, "Will the background be plain or patterned? How will it best enhance the design?"

Once the rug is under way, you must constantly test design elements by hooking a small bit of background next to the design. The point of contact between de-

There are several lovely ways to hook the background.

Hook small spirals and then fill the empty spaces between them.

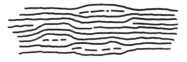

Slightly varied horizontal lines create a gentle, pleasing effect.

Scaling is an easy way to get an interesting dimension in your background.

Hook random shapes and then fill them in. This gives your background a sense of motion and activity.

This background follows the contours of the design, becoming a subtle extension of the design.

sign elements and background, the positive and negative use of space, is a vital one. It is here that problems may occur. Too often the design and background blend into each other and the line of demarcation is lost. Go to any exhibit of hooked rugs, and it is almost certain that you will see some rugs with this problem.

There are occasional exceptions, times when it is *desirable* for background and design to blend. In an area that might naturally be in shadow, such as the lower edge of a seated animal or the shadowed bases of leaves in a floral design, it is best not to emphasize the difference between design and background, because we want to draw attention to other parts of the design. But generally, it is important to prevent the design from disappearing into the background.

Sometimes a variety of related or unrelated colors are hooked "hit or miss," as each piece comes to hand, rather than according to a preconceived plan. When a large area, such as a background, is covered this way, you may choose to blend a plain color (beige, gray, or a medium value of the dominant color) with the other wools.

The fur of lions, tigers, and many cats is made up of various shades of yellows, oranges, and golds. Therefore purple, the complementary color of yellow, is an excellent color for the ground area beneath the cats. It gives the yellows a certain sparkle and helps to create attractive and harmonious color combinations.

Use wools in a variety of light colors such as peach, apricot, tan, beige, and brown and overdye them in a *weak* bright purple dye. If you need a darker ground area, use darker values of wool and a slightly stronger purple dye bath.

Getting Finished

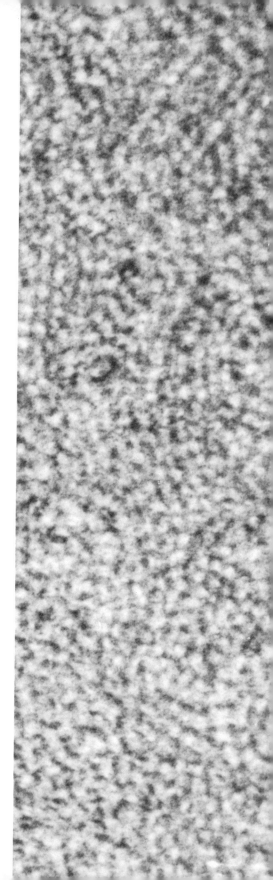

Hooking the Rug

Basic Directions

Hooking has four basic components: the hook, the strip of wool fabric, the base fabric, and your own two hands.

The base fabric, or backing, is usually a good-quality burlap, monk's cloth, or linen. The weave must be sufficiently open so that you can push the hook through it, catch the strip, and pull up a portion of the strip to form a loop. The backing must be placed in a frame to keep it taut before you can begin to hook.

Begin by pushing the hook through a mesh of the backing, sliding the smooth shank down between the forefinger and the thumb of your left hand. Let the hook catch hold of the wool strip, which is also between the forefinger and thumb. Pull the strip up, bringing the end through to the top side to a height of about 1 inch. (All the ends are pulled through to the top side. Later they will be cut off even with the pile.) Then put the hook through the next hole and pull a loop up to a height of about ⅛ inch. As you pull the strip up, press the smooth side of the hook against the burlap to make the hole bigger. Then the hook will come through without catching.

Working in any direction that seems easy for you, keep pulling up loops as evenly as you can. When the end of the strip is reached, be sure to bring it through to the top side of the backing and trim it even with the tops of the loops.

If your strips are very narrow, you will probably

___

Strip of wool

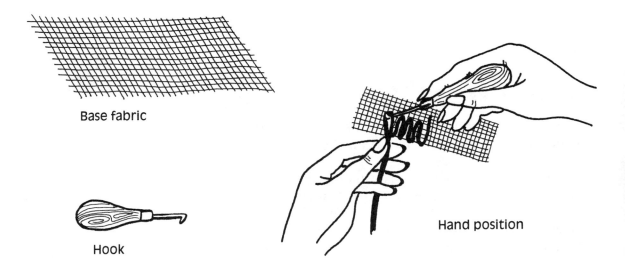

Base fabric

Hook

Hand position

The four components of hooking. Notice that the lower hand holds the strip of wool, keeping tension on it as it is pulled up through the backing.

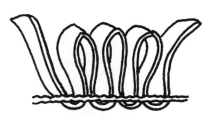

This enlarged view of the loops shows how the cut ends should be even with the tops of the loops. On the underside, the wool should be flat and smooth.

hook into almost every mesh. If your strips are wider, you can skip holes as necessary to keep the loops from being packed too tightly. The loops should touch each other comfortably so that the surface is firm. If they are packed too closely, they will strain the backing; if they are too loose, the rug will not wear well. Experience will quickly teach you.

You can practice hooking on an odd piece of backing or at the side of your pattern until you get the knack of it. Practice hooking straight lines and curved lines; then make little circles and fill them in. The underside should feel smooth to your fingertips. There shouldn't be any loops, bumps, or tails left hanging. The top surface should be even, without any open spaces. Don't expect perfection on your first project. This is your learning piece. You will probably look back on it with great affection.

In your first attempt at hooking, you may find that you are pulling out the previous loop as you hook. Don't be discouraged. This can be remedied by slightly twisting the hook away from you as you pull up. With practice you will find that you do this automatically.

The Finished Surface

The surfaces of the best rugs are thick and luxurious, but they also have "give" and flexibility. The loops form a pile that is even in height and even in density. When a rug is closely hooked with no hidden places left unhooked, dirt and sand cannot penetrate the pile. Soil sits on the surface, where it can easily be vacuumed or brushed away.

If a rug is too tightly hooked, it will tend to curl. It may be so stiff that it will not lie flat on the floor. Obviously, there will be strain on the foundation. On the other hand, if a rug is so loosely hooked that the tops of the loops don't touch each other, the backing may be visible in places. A rug that has too few loops looks skimpy and inadequate, and it certainly won't wear well. A well-hooked rug has loops that mesh; the loops in one row fit between the loops in the next rather than lining up with them. Meshing creates a close, thick texture.

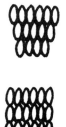

Above: Notice how the tops of the loops in the second and third rows mesh neatly in between the bottoms of the loops above them. **Below:** These unmeshed loops allow spots of backing to show through.

Styles of Hooking

Although the process of hooking is simple and straightforward, the finished pieces vary, depending on the interpretation and style developed by the rug hooker. There can be many variations of a single design. For example, a cat design could be done in a realistic style, a primitive style, or an impressionistic style.

Realistic, or tapestry, hooking uses finely cut, hand-dyed strips in a detailed design. Primitive hooking is done with wider strips and a simpler use of color values. There may be only one value in an element of the design combined with a darker or lighter value for an outline. There are variations even within these two styles: some realistic pieces are simpler than others; and some primitive pieces are more detailed than others.

Just as new styles constantly develop in the art world, new ways of painting with wool emerge among today's literate and thoughtful rug hookers. During the period prior to World War II and continuing into the fifties and sixties, a new style of rug hooking developed, which I have termed impressionistic hooking.

Many rug hookers wanted to see their art evolve beyond what was being hooked at the time. They developed new methods of hooking and discovered a palette of colors and values that had not generally been used. The new style of hooking did not have the simplicity and naïveté of the primitive rug. Neither did it have the sophistication of the realistic style that was to develop later.

The term impressionistic is, of course, related to the French Impressionists. In the late nineteenth and early twentieth centuries, the Impressionists painted landscapes, still lifes, and portraits in a highly individualistic way – not as these subjects actually were, but as the painters "saw" them. Impressionistic hooking, drawing its inspiration from these renegade painters, has developed into a beautiful style of its own.

Finishing Touches

Holidays

Before you begin to feel the fine sense of accomplishment that comes with having completed a hooked piece, there is something else you must do: turn the piece over and look for the spaces you have left unhooked. Rug hookers call these spaces *holidays*. It is rare not to find holidays in even the most carefully worked pieces. I try to fill in all the spaces as I go along, but when I turn my rug over, I am usually shocked to see how many I have missed. Of course, you'll see very narrow pieces of the rug backing here and there. You don't have to worry about them unless they are over ⅛ inch wide.

Although the unhooked spaces are obvious when you check the underside of your rug, you may not be able to see them on the top. To locate the missed spaces on the top, use several smooth toothpicks. Working on a small area at a time, poke a toothpick through each of six or seven unhooked spaces. When you carefully turn the piece over, you can identify the spaces on top by the ends of the toothpicks.

You may be thinking, "Why bother filling in the spaces when you can't even see them from the top?" Look more closely at an area where there are unfilled spaces. You will see that the loops may lean over a little instead of standing straight. And the empty spaces become traps for dirt and grit. It's best to be a little fussy now and fill them in right away.

Toothpicks pushed up from the underside of the rug help to locate holidays so that they may be filled in.

The Border

The size of a completed piece may be different from the size of its original pattern, because hooking usually causes a slight shrinkage to occur. If the finished size is critical, be prepared to add another border to the outside of the piece. The size of a pillow cover that is being hooked to cover a specific pillow or the size of upholstery for a chair must be exactly right. Another instance when size is critical is when you are hooking a rug to cover stair treads and risers. It is best to hook the pieces for treads and risers separately, especially when they are being made for stairs in an old house, where the size of the steps may well vary.

Early rug makers loved to use black borders on their rugs (as well as black outlines in their designs), probably because they had a lot of black wool to use up. The trouble with a black border is that it shows every speck of dust. It is far better to use a tweed or a mixture in a dark color that harmonizes with the colors in the rug. The texture of a tweed or mixture disguises dust.

Most rugs need a border. A light-colored rug without a border seems to float above the floor. Making the border darker than the background of the rug visually holds the rug down.

Initialing and Dating

We do our descendants a favor when we sign or initial our work and date it. You can hook the information in an inconspicuous place or you can write it on a piece of tape with an indelible pen and sew the tape to the back of the rug. One rug hooker, Ruth Twombly of Brunswick, Maine, has a fine idea. She embroiders her name and the date on the rug tape before it is sewn on. Laurel Brown of Taneytown, Maryland, uses a similar method: she embroiders her name on a piece of cotton or linen and sews it to the back of the rug.

If you choose to hook your initials and the date into the rug, make them secondary to the rug's design and coloring. The lower corners, in the border, or tucked in close to the base of the design are good locations. Pick grayed tones that are a shade lighter or darker than the background; don't use starkly contrasting colors. Make the initials small and somewhat difficult to find. The less conspicuous they are, the more fun it is to look for them.

Binding the Edges

All rugs need to be bound on the edges. The point of greatest wear on a rug is its edge; some extra care at this weakest area will pay off in future years. Two

Enjoying a cat as a pet may be beneficial to our mental health. Research has shown that children who play with cats suffer less from emotional and social problems. Sometimes, mentally ill patients who are unresponsive to people will accept affection from a pet, especially from a cat.

methods for binding edges will be discussed in this chapter. The first method is recommended for rugs that will be used as floor coverings. The second method is for hooked pieces that will be used as wall hangings or placed in areas of little traffic.

For Rugs.   Complete your hooked piece by hooking up to the outermost pattern line, putting at least two rows of hooking parallel to that line. Use long strips to make these last rows. Position the loops close to the edge of the line; hook them so that they are close together and even; and hook them slightly lower than the rest of the loops in the rug. This is especially important when a rug is hooked with wide strips. The lower loops not only help protect the edge of the rug, but they create an attractive appearance as well. On some rugs, it may take as many as four or five rows, with each row slightly lower than the previous one, to grade the pile from the regular height to a lower height.

When the hooking is completed, steam press the rug thoroughly. Then, to prevent the backing from unraveling, put a row of machine zigzag stitches (or two rows of small, straight machine stitches) about 1 inch beyond the last row of loops. Sew completely around the rug, going across the corners. It is helpful to have someone hold the rug as you stitch it. This edge stitching can also be done *before* the hooking is completed, if you are sure that the edge of the rug will be on the printed line.

Next, trim off the excess backing just beyond the stitching. Then carefully fold the backing and pin it so that about ¼ inch is visible from the right side. Insert a length of narrow cording into the fold. This strengthens the edge of the rug, which is vulnerable to wear. The edge created by the folded backing is then oversewn with knitting worsted in a matching or harmonizing color. It is oversewn completely around the rug, making a neat, strong edge.

All that is left to do is to cover the small strip of backing that is visible on the underside with rug tape.

Use rug tape that is 1¼ inches wide and sew it on by hand. Note that if you wash the tape or dye it to blend with your rug colors, you can expect it to shrink about 3 inches per yard. Finally, steam press the rug tape to complete the binding process.

For Hangings.   The second method of binding edges, recommended for decorative items and rugs that will not be subject to hard wear, dispenses with the over-sewing of yarn. *Before* you hook the rug, sew a row of zigzag stitches (or two rows of straight stitches) about 1 inch beyond the edge of the pattern. Then machine-stitch your rug tape to the outside edge of the pattern, catching the tape about ¹⁄₁₆ inch from its inside edge.

Now hook the rug, going right up to the stitching line. When the hooking is completed and the rug has been steam-pressed, cut off the excess backing just beyond the zigzag line. Then fold back the tape and the excess backing and hem them (by hand) to the back of the rug. Miter your corners carefully and avoid disturbing any of the loops.

Care and Cleaning

Hooked rugs may be vacuumed, but the power nozzles of many vacuum cleaners are too powerful to use on hand-crafted rugs. Use the regular nozzle about once a week. Or you can lightly brush the rug on a flat surface.

Even when rugs are badly soiled, don't beat them to clean them. Place dirty rugs upside down in a shady area of a lawn and gently pat them to release sand and grit before vacuuming them.

Rugs may be cleaned right on the floor. Use any good-quality foam rug cleaner, but don't scrub the rugs with a harsh brush.

Jessie Turbayne, a rug hooker who also collects and repairs old rugs, has developed a rug cleaner that she calls Heirloom Care (see Sources of Supplies in the back of this book). Each bottle of cleaner comes with a soft brush. It has become popular with rug makers who appreciate the frailties of hand-hooked rugs.

Sometimes it is convenient to take rugs outside on the lawn to clean them, but the sun can cause quick fading, no matter how well the dyeing has been done. It is best to keep your hookings away from bright light altogether.

Finishing a Silent Companion

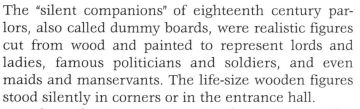

The "silent companions" of eighteenth century parlors, also called dummy boards, were realistic figures cut from wood and painted to represent lords and ladies, famous politicians and soldiers, and even maids and manservants. The life-size wooden figures stood silently in corners or in the entrance hall.

Today, silent companions are becoming popular again. Imaginative interior decorators and homemakers are adding interest to their rooms with these quiet figures. Rug hookers, who "paint with wool," can create their own hooked versions of silent companions – and what better subject than a friendly cat?

You may want to make one of the projects in this book, such as "Two Cats on a Pillow," into a silent companion. In this chapter, you will learn how to strengthen the edges of your hooking, how to cut it to shape, and how to mount it on a wooden backing so that it can stand free or lean against a wall.

Materials Needed

Dye
White glue (like Elmer's Glue-All)
Old newspapers
White paper towels
Brown paper
Small watercolor brush
Single-edge razor blades (or an X-Acto knife)
1¼-inch rug tape, enough to cover the bottom
   edge of the piece, in a harmonizing color
¼-inch plywood, a little larger than the design

Outlining

Outlines are not usually used in hooked pieces, except in primitives, but an outline is essential for the freestanding figure of a silent companion. Without a strong outline, the figure may disappear into the background behind it, into the wallpaper, furniture, and accessories that surround it.

Nevertheless, the color of the outline must not compete with the primary color of the hooked figure. Choose a harmonizing color that is a dull color with gray in it. For "Two Cats on a Pillow," I chose a dull brown. The brown harmonized with the colors in the cats, but it was sufficiently different from their colors to keep the cats visually separate from the edging color. At the same time, the brown wasn't so bright that it would be too obvious.

Hook three or four rows of the color you choose all around the hooked design – except at the base of the figure, which will be finished with tape. Make the final two rows of loops as low as possible so that they won't lean over. Using a damp cloth, steam press the edging rows on the wrong side.

Cut the strips of wool as long as possible for the edging rows – or use yarn. I prefer to use yarn because it is continuous; there are no ends to worry about at this vulnerable edge. See Basic Dyeing for tips on dyeing yarn to match.

Finishing the Edges

The finished edges of a hooked figure must be as inconspicuous as possible. Begin by preparing a double-strength dye solution, the same color that was used for the hooked outline. Place your hooked piece right side up on a ¼-inch-thick pad of newspaper. Use a small paintbrush to apply the dye solution to the burlap backing as close to the hooked loops as you can, making it about ¼ inch wide. After painting a few inches of burlap, use a folded pad of paper towels to sop up the excess dye. Continue to paint all the edges of the hooking except the base of the figure.

Before applying dye to the reverse side of the backing, lay some clean brown paper on top of the newspapers to protect your hooking from any ink that might rub off the newspaper. Then put the hooking face down on the clean pad. Paint the backing on the reverse side of the hooking in the same way you painted the front. Sop up the excess moisture as you did before, pressing hard with clean paper towels. The pressing helps force the dye to penetrate the fibers of the backing.

In order to do a good job, take your time applying the dye. It may require several applications to obtain the right color. When you have finished, remove the brown paper and place the hooking face up on the pad of newspapers. Let it dry thoroughly for a few hours or overnight.

The next step in finishing the edges is to prevent the burlap backing from unraveling. To strengthen the burlap, apply a line of white glue (about ⅛ inch wide) directly next to the last row of hooking. Don't be alarmed if the glue touches the loops. It may look terrible for a moment, but the glue will shrink and become transparent as it dries.

As you apply the glue, pay particular attention to the corners. It is also a good idea to rub the tip of the glue applicator on the backing to force the glue to penetrate the fibers at these vulnerable points.

After letting the glue dry for an hour, apply a second line of glue to the reverse side of the backing. Remember to protect the front of your hooking from printer's ink by covering the newspaper pad with clean brown paper. Let the glue on the back dry for an hour.

The final step in finishing the edges requires cutting off the excess burlap. You may cringe at the thought of cutting the backing, but believe me, the glue really will hold the burlap edges in place.

It is best to work from the back side of the hooked

piece to cut the excess burlap. Use a very sharp razor blade or X-Acto knife. Cut about ⅛ inch from the last row of hooking – just outside the line of white glue. Cut all around the design except at the base of the figure.

After you have cut the burlap, apply white glue to the edge of the cut burlap. If the glue beads as you apply it, smooth it out with your finger. Let the glue dry completely.

Finish the base of the figure – the bottom edge of the hooking – by cutting the burlap about 1 inch from the last row of hooking. Then turn the burlap back and hand-sew 1¼-inch tape to cover it.

Building the Wooden Stand

To finish your silent companion, you will need to cut a piece of ¼-inch plywood in the same shape as your hooked piece. If necessary, you can ask your local lumberyard to do this for you. First, make a paper pattern. Lay the completed hooked figure on a large piece of paper, and weight it with several heavy objects, such as old flatirons or heavy bookends. Then carefully trace around the edges with a pencil. Remove the hooked work and draw a second outline ¼ inch inside your tracing. Cut out the pattern on the inside line.

Tape the paper pattern to the plywood and trace it. Then you can cut the plywood with an electric ½-inch saber saw, and sand the edges smooth.

To reinforce the stand and help keep it from warping, cut a length of 1- by 2-inch lumber and center it on the plywood stand perpendicular to the base. Screw it into place from the right side of the plywood stand, and countersink the screws. You may want to attach a handle to this piece to make the stand easy to move and carry.

If you want your silent companion to be freestanding, use hinges to attach two scraps of plywood to the back of the base of the stand. Mount the hinged pieces at just less than a 90-degree angle. The finished base will work just like the supporting base on a stand-up paper doll.

You can paint the entire piece in a dull, harmonizing color if you like.

Mounting the Silent Companion

A good way to attach the hooked piece to the stand is to use strips of double-faced tape. Attach the strips of tape down the length of the stand, and then carefully lay the hooked piece on top. Weight it down with two or three heavy objects for a few hours. Then stand back and admire your silent companion.

Joan Leith Moshimer.

The Hooked Cat

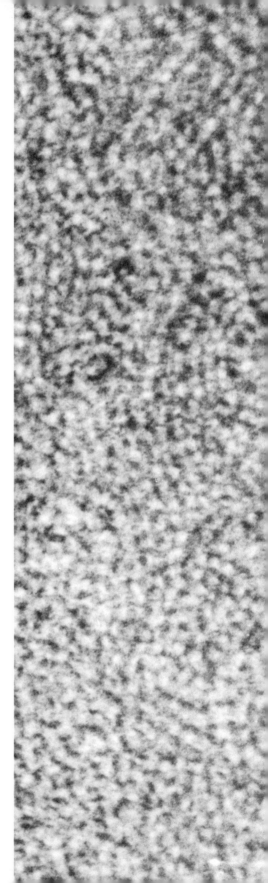

Specific to Cats

Designing a Cat Rug

To draw a cat, we need to look closely at the face. The most fascinating feature of a cat's face is its eyes. The expression of the eyes is important in achieving the likeness of a cat. We need to consider how we want the eyes to look at the very beginning of a project. If the pupil of a cat's eye is a thin slit, it will convey a different expression than if the pupil is large and round. The heavy-lidded eyes of a sleepy lion are completely different from the piercing look of a hunting lioness or of a snarling tiger.

We also need to consider the set of a cat's ears. The ears may point forward in an alert manner; they may be pulled back, betraying uncertainty; they may be flattened to show anger; or they may be held extremely flat against the head to show aggression. (It is easy to understand that in a fight, ears are less likely to be injured if they are held flat against the head.)

Whiskers, too, play a subtle role in expression. In an alert, friendly animal, the whiskers tend to swing forward; they appear extended and fairly straight. When a cat is sleeping or is relaxed and contented, the whiskers are more "laid back." Sometimes the whiskers are pulled back when a cat is suspicious or uncertain. You may want to experiment with the position of the whiskers to achieve the expression you want.

Designing a cat's nose is easy once you realize that the basic shape is a triangle. Make sure the size of the nose is in scale with the rest of the face, especially

*A cat's eyes and ears hold the key to his moods. **Above:** A cat with pricked ears and wide-open, rounded eyes has an alert, friendly expression. **Below:** We can read this cat's suspicious attitude from his slightly flattened ears and narrowed eyes. His upper eyelids have dropped to partially cover his pupils.*

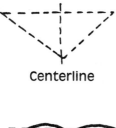

Centerline

Centerline

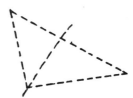

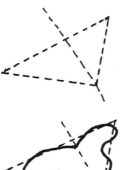

Drawing the nose of a cat facing to one side is essentially the same as drawing the front-view nose. The centerline of your original triangle will be diagonal rather than vertical, so the triangle is skewed. Notice that the nostril opening on the far side is smaller than the one on the near side.

The basic shape of the cat's nose is a triangle. For a front-view nose, draw a triangle that is wider along the top than the sides. Next, draw two curving lines across the top. Extend the outer curves of those lines as shown to form two nostrils. Finally, continue the curves in graceful lines that meet at the point of the triangle.

with the eyes. A safe guide for most cats is to make the width of the top line of the triangle about three-quarters the width of one eye.

You will be able to draw a front view of a cat's nose fairly easily. If the cat is facing slightly to one side, you will need to draw the nose a little larger on one side than on the other to make a correct side view. Before drawing the details, experiment by drawing the basic triangles until you get one that looks right. Then you can proceed with the details. Note that the far side of the triangle is shorter than the near side. The top line is somewhat foreshortened, too. And the nostril opening on the far side is smaller. Compare the illustrations for drawing a cat's nose from a front view and from a side view.

In primitive hooking, we seldom see such niceties as nostrils or natural colors in cats' noses. Often the nose is just a dark spot. Sometimes the nose can be omitted altogether.

When cats are portrayed in imaginative, fantastic ways, their noses can be made any shape you like. I sometimes use a heart for the fancy cat's nose.

Hooking the Flow of Fur

The more realistic you want your cat to appear, the more you will need to be aware of the flow of the fur. The face is where the flow of fur begins. Look closely at your cat's face. You can see that the hairs are shorter on the face, and the direction in which the hair grows varies dramatically, especially on the nose. At the inner corners of the eyes, the flow of the fur radiates in all directions – outward, upward, and downward. Notice how the tiny hairs swing upward on the bridge of the nose and then downward toward the nostril area. Those velvety hairs form intricate patterns as

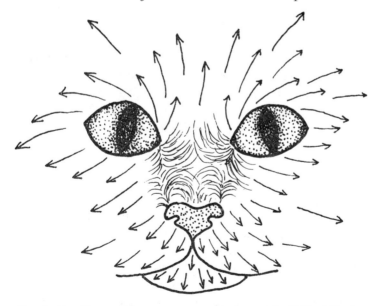

Study the flow of fur on your cat's face. You'll find that the hairs on the bridge of the nose create intricate, swirling designs, which you'll want to reproduce in your hooking.

they follow the contours of the face, fanning out and spreading in graceful arcs like the eddies in a stream that separate and rejoin. The face is the starting point of the flow of fur. From there the stream of fur flows down the spine, and then from the spine it curves down on the sides, the tail, and the legs.

Of course, rug hookers won't be hooking every hair, but it's helpful to be aware of the way the hair normally grows, especially if you are hooking a large cat or a closeup of a cat's face. Even when you're hooking a smaller cat, paying attention to the flow of fur will make your cat look more real and interesting.

Hooking a Tiger Cat

When you are hooking a tiger or tabby cat, which has variegated markings on its face and body and a variety of changing colors, it is essential to hook in short lines in order to make the color changes. (The only exception would be when you are hooking a long-haired cat.) Be sure to hook in a generally downward direction on the body and legs.

The facial markings on a tiger cat give a wonderful variety of expressions. To capture the markings as you hook, begin by identifying the lightest and darkest areas. Squint your eyes to do this. Once the light and dark areas are identified and hooked in, you can easily add the in-between values.

Hooking a Primitive Cat

If you are hooking a primitive cat, using the outline-and-fill method, you may disregard the flow of fur and detailed facial expression. In fact, the eyes and nose are usually shown by simple spots of wool. To outline and fill, simply use one color of wool for an outline and a harmonizing or contrasting color to fill in the outlined areas. Either the outline or the inner area can be done in a tweed or check to give textural interest.

It is not always necessary to outline. Dorothy Marosy's pensive cat in "Cat Scan" and the fiddling cat in "Cow Jumping over Moon" (see the color section of this book) have no need of outlines. There is plenty of contrast between the cats and the backgrounds behind them.

Hooking Whiskers

To hook the whiskers or not to hook them – that is the question. The trend nowadays is *not* to hook them. For a wall hanging, a pillow, or a hooked piece that will have only a decorative use, the whiskers can be added after the piece is hooked. Whiskers can be made of nylon fishing line, yarn, horsehair, thread, or even shed cat whiskers.

Nylon fishing line can be anchored on the reverse side of the hooking. But fishing line is transparent and difficult to see. It also has a way of sticking out in all directions in an unnatural way. When yarn is used, it has to be constantly adjusted to keep it in position; and yarn has a limp look. Horsehair from a horse's tail works fairly well, but for most of us, it is not readily available. Even if we have access to horses, the white or light-colored hair we need for whiskers is rare.

White or pale gray heavy-duty thread can be used for whiskers. Rub a little liquid starch into the lengths of thread after they are stitched in place. Then pull them into shape with your fingers as they dry.

But what could be more perfect than real cat whiskers? They have the right curves, and they are heavy at the base, tapering to a fine tip. Since we had a large family of cats, we often came upon whiskers that had fallen out. The best way I know to anchor them to your hooking is to use a white glue, like Elmer's glue. Separate the loops in the places where you want to position the whiskers and apply glue to each place. Attach the base of the whisker to the spot of glue and hold it in place for a few minutes until the glue dries.

You don't need to follow nature so faithfully that

*In his interesting book, **Your Incredible Cat,** David Green describes the ability of cats to sense an imminent disaster. Scientists think that cats can detect positively charged atoms in the atmosphere. An increased number of these atoms are released immediately before an earthquake. Cats detect the difference in the atmosphere and race back and forth, scratching furiously to be let outside a house or building. Their behavior can be understood as an urgent warning of impending disaster. Peasants living near Italy's Mount Vesuvius recognize their cats' restless behavior as a warning that the volcano is about to erupt.*

you include as many whiskers as cats really have. Three to five whiskers on each side of the cat's face usually looks good.

When a hooked piece is going to be used on the floor, the whiskers can be hooked in, embroidered, or simply indicated by hooked spots on the cheeks of the cat. If you decide to hook the whiskers, they should be hooked first, and the loops should be slightly higher than the surrounding loops, so that the whiskers won't get lost. Use close, even loops that will hold their line when the surrounding loops are hooked.

Cat Colors

This chapter contains detailed directions for dyeing strips to be used in hooking cats – from Siamese cats to calico cats. But first it might be helpful to make some general comments about cat colors.

The Colors on a Cat's Face

When you are choosing the colors for a cat's eyes, you may use artistic license and make them any color you like, or you can follow the suggestions given later in this chapter. If two colors are suggested, you may want to combine the colors, using the darker color close to the pupil. Note that kittens have gray-blue eyes, which will change to their adult color at the time of their weaning. Strong eye liners and other markings around their eyes make kittens' eyes appear large.

You may want to outline a cat's eyes with a thin strip of tightly woven black wool or some black yarn, unless the cat is white or a very light color. In that case, black would be too stark; it would provide too much contrast. Try medium gray or a darker gray to outline the eyes on a light-colored cat. If black is too stark for the pupils of the eyes, you can use an off-black, sometimes called antique black.

Many cats' noses can be hooked in dull brownish pinks or soft, grayed tones – pinkish grays and plain grays. Burmese cats may have rich brown noses, and Himalayan and Siamese cats may have dark, brownish-gray noses.

If the nose color matches the color of the cat's fur,

then you will need to make the nose either darker or lighter than the fur color. The nose should not be too brightly colored or too obvious; yet, at the same time, it shouldn't get lost and be almost impossible to find. Never outline the nose in black. It will look too harsh. If you want to outline, dark or medium grays will probably work.

Of course, you can also make the noses different colors than nature intended if you like.

If you are hooking a cat's whiskers, white or pale gray is usually right, although the whiskers on a very light cat should be darker.

Gathering the Colors for Fur

After you have made several rugs or after you have acquired a treasury of old wools, it is easy to choose a range of colors from light to dark that could blend together well for hooking a realistic cat. It's an exciting process for experienced hookers. Beginners, who are unlikely to have a backlog of leftovers from other projects, may gain some ideas from the following suggested combinations.

For a *calico cat,* use any of the following combinations:

□ cream, pale yellow, beige, dark tan, medium brown, and darker gray-brown
□ pale yellow, soft orange, light rust, dark rust, and dark brown
□ off-white, pale gray, light orange, medium gray, dark gray, and off-black
□ pale gray, warm beige, light brown, medium gray, and medium-dark gray
□ cream, pale golden yellow, medium golden yellow, burnt orange, rust, and medium brown-rust

For a *Siamese cat,* combine white, cream, warm orange-yellow, light brown, medium gray-brown, brown-black.

For a *black cat,* combine black and several grays, from medium-light gray to dark gray.

For a *smokey gray cat,* combine medium gray and
two or three lighter and darker values of gray.

For a *white cat,* combine a small amount of white
and plenty of off-whites – eggshell-white, light beige,
medium beige, warm gray, and gray-beige.

Formulas for Dyeing Cat Colors

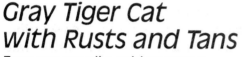

Gray Tiger Cat with Rusts and Tans
Eyes are usually gold or green.

Dye Solutions for Dip-Dyeing
#1 = 1/4 t. Tan in 1/2 cup boiling water
#2 = 3/4 t. Silver Gray in 1 1/2 cups boiling water
Add 1 T. of white vinegar to each dye bath before
dipping the wool.

Wools
Four or more pieces of off-white wool, each 10
inches by 15 inches.
The wool pieces should be dipped lengthwise.
The pieces will be referred to as **A**, **B**, **C**, and **D**.
A will blend from medium-light grays to me-
dium-light tan-rusts.
B will blend from medium-dark gray to medium
rusts.
C will blend from light grays to medium grays.
D will blend from medium grays to dark grays.

To obtain A: Use a dye bath with 1 t. of the #1 solution. Dip one end of the wool piece a little more than
halfway into the dye bath. Don't allow the deepest end
of the piece to become darker than a medium-light
value.

Then make a dye bath using 1 T. of the #2 solution.
Dip the other end of the wool a little over halfway into

the solution, again allowing the deepest end to reach only a medium-light value.

There will be a blend of tan and gray in the middle of this wool piece with medium tan-rusts at one end and medium-light grays at the other end. Set this piece aside.

To obtain B: Use a dye bath with 2 t. of the #1 solution. Dip one end of the piece of wool a little over halfway into the bath, keeping the deepest end no darker than a medium value.

Then make a dye bath with 2 T. of the #2 solution. Dip the other end of the wool a little over halfway into the solution, dyeing the deepest part a medium-dark value.

This piece will also have a blend of tan and gray in the middle, but there will be darker tones of tan-rusts at one end and darker tones of gray at the other end. Set this piece aside.

To obtain C: Use a dye bath with 2 t. of the #1 solution and 1½ T. of the #2 solution. Dip the wool piece about three-fourths of the way into the dye bath. You should get medium grays at the dark end and medium-light values at the middle. Then, as the dye bath weakens, dip the piece all the way into the bath to obtain light values at the top of the piece.

The grays will be slightly different from the grays in A and B. Set this piece aside.

To obtain D: Use a dye bath with 3 t. of the #2 solution and 1 T. of the #1 solution. Dip the wool piece as you did to obtain C. You should get dark grays at the deepest end, medium-dark grays in the middle, and medium gray at the upper end.

These grays will be slightly different from the others you have obtained, giving you a nice range from which to choose.

After you have dyed A, B, C, and D, mix about ½ cup hot water with ⅛ cup of vinegar in a flat 10- by 15-inch pan. Lay the D wool flat in the pan with the vinegar water. Add 1 T. salt. Put a white paper towel over the piece of wool.

Then layer the other wool pieces over the paper towel in this order: *B* wool, salt, a paper towel; *A* wool, salt, a paper towel; and lastly, *C* wool and 1 T. of salt. Pour 1 cup of hot water mixed with ¼ cup of vinegar over all the pieces. Press the wool down gently with your fingers to make sure that all the pieces are thoroughly saturated. Then cover the pan with foil and simmer for 45 minutes. (For a pan this size, heavy-duty foil that is 18 inches wide works well.) Or you can place the pan in a 350° oven for 15 minutes, followed by 45 minutes at 300°.

The leftover dyes can be used to give some useful off-shades that will add character to your hookings. Select some harmonizing tweeds; they can be any size you have available. For this tiger cat I'd use some brown/rust/tan tweed, some dark gray/light gray tweed, and a dull orange tweed. Presoak the tweeds in Ivory water, lay a few of the pieces in a pan, and pour some of the leftover dyes over them. Sprinkle a couple of tablespoons of salt over the pieces. Then add another layer of tweeds, more leftover dye, and more salt until all of the dye is used. If you think it is needed, add enough hot tap water to prevent the wool from drying out when it cooks. Cover the pan and bake it for 350 degrees F. for 15 minutes and at 300 degrees F. for another 45 minutes. Check after half an hour to see whether you need to add more water. Then rinse the wool pieces as described in Basic Dyeing.

Gray Tiger Cat
Eyes are usually gold or green.

Dye Solutions for Dip-Dyeing
#1 = as for *Gray Tiger Cat with Rusts and Tans*
#2 = as for *Gray Tiger Cat with Rusts and Tans*

Wools
Light tan or beige wools (like Dorr's background wools #42 or #31) for *A* and *B* pieces. Off-white wool for *D*.

Follow the dyeing directions for *Gray Tiger Cat with Rusts and Tans* with the following exceptions.

To obtain A: Use a dye bath with 1 T. plus 1 t. of the #2 solution. Omit using the #1 solution altogether. Dip tan or beige wool all the way into the solution to get a medium-light value at one end of the piece up to light values at the other end.

To obtain B: Use a dye bath with 2 T. plus 2 t. of the #2 solution. Omit using the #1 solution. Dip tan or beige wool all the way into the solution to get dark values at one end of the piece and medium values at the other end.

Omit C.

To obtain D: Follow the directions for obtaining *D* for the *Gray Tiger Cat with Rusts and Tans.* Use off-white wool.

To use the leftover dyes, follow the directions given for *Gray Tiger Cat with Rusts and Tans,* using several light to medium gray tweeds.

Black Cat
Eyes are usually gold or green.

If you have a selection of medium and dark gray wools, some off-blacks, and a small amount of black, you won't need to dye to make a black cat. Most black cats look best in off-blacks, which are not real blacks but extremely dark colors – blue-blacks or brown-blacks. A black cat seen in bright sunlight may actually have a coat of very dark browns.

You will only need a small amount of pure black for the deepest shadows. To show the light that the smooth, shiny coat of a black cat reflects, you will need some medium and medium-light grays. These help to portray shape and form, too.

If the black cat you are planning has some white on him, you will need white, of course, and some gray-whites and medium grays. Where black and white meet, there are usually some black hairs and white hairs intermingled; the grays will help at these places. Or something that works even better, if you're lucky enough to find it, is some very fine black and white or dark gray and white tweed.

Brown-Black Cat
Eyes are usually gold or green.

Dye Solution for Dip-Dyeing
¹/₄ t. Black and
¹/₈ t. Dark Brown in ¹/₂ cup boiling water

Wools
Off-white wool

If you choose to dye the wool for a black cat, follow the directions for dip-dyeing in Basic Dyeing. For 10-by 15-inch wool pieces, add 2 T. of dye solution to the dye bath. Dip the pieces more than halfway into the solution so that you obtain very dark values on the deepest end of the wool and medium to medium-light values on the other end. (Add more dye solution if necessary.)

When working with such dark values, you will need to check the depth of color often. Squeeze as much moisture out of the wool as possible, and examine it under a good light. You want to obtain values that appear to be black but that aren't really black, so be sure to have some pure black available for comparison – even if it is an example of black in a magazine photograph.

Blue-Black Cat
Eyes are usually gold or green.

Follow the directions for a *Brown-Black Cat,* only substitute a formula of ⅜ t. Black mixed with ¹/₃₂ t. Navy
Blue for the dye solution.

Smokey Gray Cat
Eyes are usually dark orange or gold.

Dye Solution for Dip-Dyeing
1/2 t. plus 1/8 t. Taupe
1/4 t. Silver Gray in 1 cup boiling water

Wools
Off-white and beige wool (like Dorr's #31 wool)

A warm gray is needed for these beautiful creatures. And since these cats are characterized by their smooth, silky coats, it is important not to dye over any tweeds or mixtures.

Follow the directions for dip-dyeing in Basic Dyeing. You will want to obtain mostly medium values (for the bulk of the cat), some medium-light values, and only a small amount of dark values.

Slate Gray Cat
Eyes are usually copper, orange, or gold.

Dye Solution for Dip-Dyeing
1/2 t. Dark Gray and
1/2 t. Taupe in 1 cup boiling water

Wools
Off-white wool

A slate gray cat is similar to a smokey gray cat, except that the colors are not so warm; there is more neutral gray.

Dip the wool pieces for medium-dark values, as well as for medium values and small amounts of dark values.

Creamy Tan-Gold Cat

Eyes are usually hazel (light brown to a strong, yellow-brown), green, or pale gold.

Dye Solution for Dip-Dyeing
1/4 t. Ecru and
1/4 t. Champagne in 1 cup boiling water

Wools
Off-white wool and some pale gray or tan tweeds
for soft, dull textural values; or pale gold or
yellow wool for brighter cats

These cats are generally light-colored. Dip for light and medium values and lesser amounts of dark values. You will not need any really dark values.

Bobcat and Mountain Lion
Eyes usually match the brighter tones of the animals' coats.

Dye Solution for Dip-Dyeing
Same as dye solution for *Creamy Tan-Gold Cat*

Wools
Off-white wool, light brown wool (like Dorr's #5), and gray wool (like Dorr's #8218)

For bobcats or mountain lions, use the same dye solution that was used for creamy tan-gold cats, only dip for mostly dark values, as well as for medium and light values.

White Cat

Eyes are usually blue or turquoise—sometimes they are light gold.

Dye Solution for Dip-Dyeing
Same as dye solution for *Creamy Tan-Gold Cat*

Wools
Off-white wool

A white cat needs very subtle values of color. Use plain off-white wool for the lightest areas on the cat; use pure white for occasional highlights. When you dye wool to use for small amounts of shading, use the same dye solution that is used for a creamy tan-gold cat. Dip for off-white and very pale values with medium values (no dark values) at the end of the wool piece.

You might want to substitute very weak Dark Gray for the shadows. Or, if you prefer a warmer gray for shadows, use the dye solution that is given for a smokey gray cat. Dye only for medium values, and leave lots of off-white. Use pure white for highlights.

Ginger Cat or Orange Cat
Eyes are usually dark orange, gold, or green.

Dye Solution for Dip-Dyeing
1/4 t. Golden Brown and
1/4 t. Rust in 1 cup boiling water

Wools
Off-white wool for a light-colored cat; add gray
   wool and gray-brown tweeds for a dark
   orange cat

Dip for medium values for a light-colored cat. Dip
for darker values for a cat with a dark orange coat with
few light areas.

Calico Cat
Eyes are usually copper, dark orange, gold, or hazel.

Dye Solution for Dip-Dyeing
#1 = ¹/₈ t. Orange and
    ¹/₃₂ t. Taupe in 1 cup of boiling water
#2 = ¹/₃₂ t. Black in 1 cup of boiling water

Wools
Off-white wool

Calico cats, or tortoiseshell cats, are multi-colored with orange, white, gray, and black. Sometimes the blacks and grays are well blended with the orange. These cats are sometimes strikingly beautiful. Occasionally, when the colors on their faces are distributed unevenly, they have a comical air, as if they had been spotted with paint. There are often sharp divisions of color in their coats, but it doesn't hurt to blur the changes somewhat with in-between tones – grays between the black and white, light oranges between the orange and white, black-orange tones between the black and orange. You should stagger these changes.

Dip the first pieces of wool in the #1 solution. Dip for light values at the top of the strip with medium-light values in the middle and medium values at the deepest end. Then, to obtain some darker values, dip some of the pieces in the #2 solution. Try to get medium-light values at the top, medium values in the middle, and medium-dark values at the deepest end of the wool piece.

Dip a third set of wool pieces all the way to the top for medium and medium-dark values. Then add some #2 solution to the dye bath and dip the lower end again to get some dark values.

Finally, add more #2 solution to the dye bath and dip a fresh piece of wool. Go for black at one end with some dark grays in the center and light grays at the top.

Tiger
Eyes are usually copper or dark orange.

Follow the dyeing instructions for a *Calico Cat,* dyeing over off-white and tan wool, but dye the last piece solid black, instead of a range of grays and blacks. These colors will give you a fairly bright tiger. For softer, burnt oranges, substitute for #1 a solution of ¼ t. Rust, ¼ t. Golden Brown, and ¼ t. Maize in 1 cup of boiling water. (You can also use this weaker, rustier formula to get a softer, less orange calico cat.)

Siamese Cat
Eyes are usually sapphire blue.

Dye Solutions for Dip-Dyeing
#1 = ¹/₁₆ t. Old Ivory and
      ¹/₃₂ t. Ecru in 1 cup boiling water
#2 = ¹/₂ t. Dark Brown and
      ¹/₄ t. Khaki Drab in 2 cups boiling water

Wools
Off-white wool

Dyeing colors for the slender, exotic Siamese is fascinating because of the elegant colors in its coat. A Siamese cat has light to white tones and a few medium tones before the colors change quickly to dark tones. This Siamese has some creamy light values, shading to weak rosy browns, and it has rich dark browns for the points.

Dip #1 until you get a medium light color at the lower end of the wool and white at the other end. Make sure that you dye plenty of the extremely light tones. Reserve one or two of these pieces to use "as is."

The other pieces will be dipped in the #2 solution. This is a strong dye solution, and we want only weak amounts of the rosy brown over the light creamy tones that we obtained by using #1. So first we will dye only the light areas of our pieces in a weak dye bath. (We will dye the dark ends later.)

To make a weak dye bath, you may want to use only 1 t. of dye solution in the dye bath. You must use your own judgment, of course, because only you know how much wool you are dyeing.

Dip the strips of wool into the dye bath only about three-fourths of the way up the strip. After you have finished dyeing the light values, you can concentrate on getting the dark, rich browns for the Siamese points. Add approximately 2 T. of dye solution to the dye bath. Then dip the dark ends of your pieces into the boiling dye bath to a depth of about 1½ inches. Gently move the wool up and down as you wait for a rich color to develop. The dye bath will be very dark and will not clear, but as you note the solution weakening a little, dip the pieces deeper – to a depth of about 3 inches.

When all the pieces have been dyed, put any leftover dye into the dye bath and add a last piece of wool, either gray or brown. This will give you an extra dark value, which may prove to be useful. The wool should be presoaked before you add it to the dye bath. Then, after you have added a little salt, the wool can be simmered in a covered pan for 45 minutes.

Set the dip-dyed pieces as directed, but in two separate lots of light and dark pieces.

Siamese with Brown Points

To obtain good colors for a Siamese with brown points, change the #2 solution by using equal amounts of Dark Brown and Khaki Drab.

Projects for Beginners

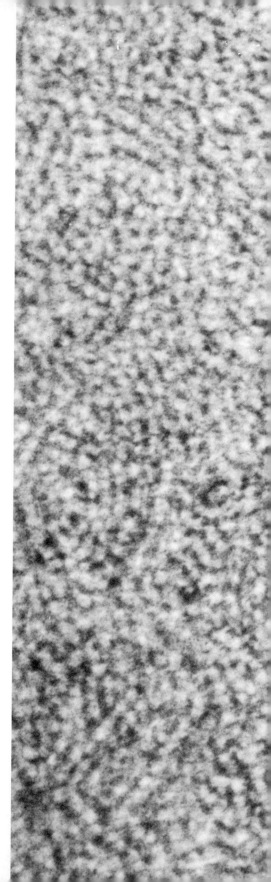

Four Kittens

This pattern was made for an 18-inch pillow, but the size can be adjusted to cover a square pillow of any dimensions. Look for a pillow whose covering will match or harmonize with the colors you want to use in the hooking, since you will be covering only one side. The pillow's cord edging will also show.

A simple design such as this is within the reach of those who are just starting out in hooking, but it will also appeal to the more experienced, especially those who have acquired a treasury of colors and tweeds.

Copy the pattern directly onto your backing if you like, or draw it freehand onto paper and trace the kitten four times on your backing, or enlarge the printed pattern to the size you require.

Cut the wool in $5/32$-inch strips, or a #5 cut.

Colors

As shown in the color photo, "Four Kittens" makes use of three as-is tweeds in harmonizing blues plus some leftover spot-dyed blue-green wools.

The accent color rose appears in the center heart and as a single line that surrounds the entire pattern. A single row of light blue divides the four squares.

Background colors are off-white and light tan.

Hooking

Hook the heart and kittens first. Next, proceed with the rows that outline the squares.

Cats seem to know our moods by the smallest changes in our voices, facial expressions, or body language. They appear to know when we are not feeling our best, and they show their affection by licking our hands. For cats, licking is an important element of healing.

Four Kittens

Fill in the background.

Before hooking the border, figure exactly how wide it must be to fit your pillow. Also examine the edges of the pillow: the corners are probably not sharp, so you will want to round the corners of your hooked work to match.

Finishing

Carefully and thoroughly steam-press the piece on the back side. Allow it to dry overnight.

Turn the excess burlap to the back side and steam-press it. Keep the fold as close to the last row of hooking as possible, so that no burlap shows from the right side.

Sew the hooked piece to the pillow by hand in a matching color of thread.

Tiger Cat

As few as ten colors are needed to hook this friendly feline: you may easily find all the wools you need in your treasury of scrap wools. Enlarge the pattern so that the finished size will measure 16 inches by 20 inches. "Tiger Cat" can then be mounted in a standard 16- by 20-inch frame for a fine decorative accent in your home.

Use ⅛-inch strips, or a #4 cut.

Colors

As pictured in the color photo, the cat is a brown tiger, but you can easily create a yellow or gray tiger cat by substituting other colors.

Use black for all the solid black areas in the pattern, as well as for the heavy lines around the mouth, eyes, and nostrils (except across the top).

1	black
2	dark brown
3	medium brown
4	dark beige
5	light beige
6	peach
7	pale gray
8	medium gray
9	dark rose
10	medium rose
11	light rose
12	white
X	bright yellow-green

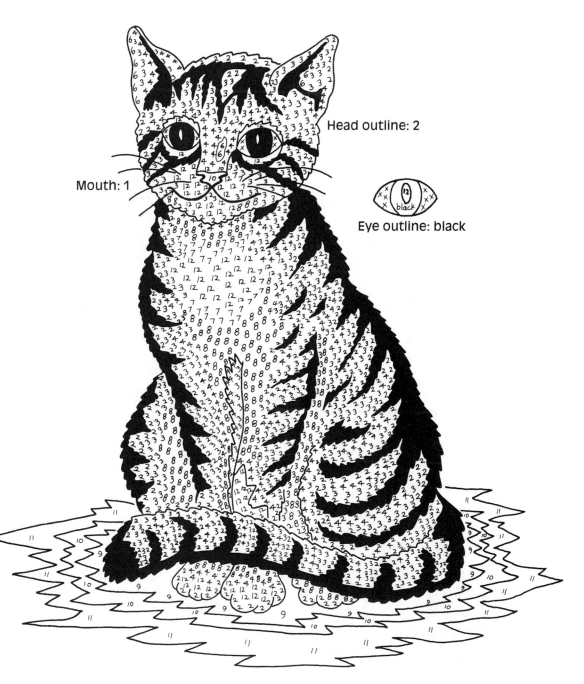

Head outline: 2

Mouth: 1

Eye outline: black

Tiger Cat

Use rose wools for the background. Or leave the backing unhooked if you prefer.

Hooking

If you plan to leave the background unhooked, remember to pull the loops lower at the outside edge of the cat and base. Loops of regular height tend to lean over slightly at the edge, distorting the shapes of the pattern. Hook the last row just inside the line.

Face and Head.   Start by hooking the eyes. Pull two long threads from a strip of black wool and twist them together. Use this strand to outline the eyes. Pull the loops high; they will later be trimmed.

Next, hook the black pupils with their white highlights. Hook the rest of the eyes in bright yellow-green.

Hook the white areas above and below the eyes.

Now, using sharp-pointed shears, trim the high black loops you hooked with the double thread for a fine, even line.

Hook the black outline around the mouth and nostrils. Use a few loops of rose at the end of the nose and hook a line of white above it.

Hook the black areas of the forehead and ears, then fill in the head according to the numbers on the pattern.

Hook the whiskers in white. A cat's whiskers are always gracefully curved, so take care to preserve their line, especially when filling in the fur behind them.

Last, hook the small spot at the base of each whisker in dark brown.

Body.   Hook the tail. Use dark brown to establish the irregular line at the top edge of the tail.

Hook the black areas and then fill in the rest of the tail, following the numbers on the pattern.

Hook the cat's chest and left front leg.

A story is told of a small girl who was struck by a car and lay in a coma for months. Medical science was unable to help her. One day a stray cat was discovered next to the inert girl in bed, patiently licking her thumb. The little cat was dirty and unkempt, and the girl's mother was horrified. But as she leaned over to remove the cat, she stopped in amazement. Her daughter's thumb had moved slightly under the gentle persistence of the cat's rough tongue. That slight movement was the first movement the child had made since the accident. The cat was allowed to stay, and a week later, the child opened her eyes. She went on to recover completely. The cat had acted on its natural instinct to lick and accomplished what the doctors couldn't do. (Experts say that there is a strong link between skin stimulation and brain activity.)

Hook the right front leg.
Complete the haunches and flanks.
Finish with the feet.

Base.   Sit the cat on a rose-colored base. Modulate the shade from dark through medium to light, as shown in the photograph.

Background.   Hook the background, working from the cat to the outside of the piece.

Finishing

Thoroughly steam-press "Tiger Cat" from the wrong side and allow it to dry overnight.

Remove the glass from a 16- by 20-inch frame; it will not be used.

Cut heavy cardboard to fit. Center the hooked piece over it and secure it with pins.

Using a darning needle and long pieces of heavy thread, sew the piece to the cardboard. Keep the piece smooth so that it will lie flat when you are finished.

Fit the mounted piece into the frame.

Lion and Lamb

This rug can be hooked with leftovers and as-is wools. To meld the values, use the no-dye overdye method of simmering related colors (see Overdyeing for Beauty).

Cut the wool in $3/16$-inch strips, or a #6 cut.

Lion and Lamb

Colors

Lion. A camel's-hair or camel-colored coat works perfectly for the lion. For the magnificent mane that frames his face, select tweeds and other leftovers in somewhat bright tones of both dark brown and light brown.

You'll also need small amounts of rusty brown and grayed brown.

Cub. Use slightly orangy-tan wools.

Lamb. Select black and gray tweeds for the lamb's head and legs.

For the fleece, a pure white will be too stark, so look for grayed and creamy whites.

As pictured, the lamb was hooked with wool of a cream and pale-peach check. The fabric, from an old coat, was very loosely woven and had to be shrunk before it could be cut. I machine-washed it in very hot water, then plunged it into ice-cold water and machine-dried it on the hottest setting. These efforts worked so well that the fabric thickened up almost too much. The surface of the hooking appears raised slightly – not an unrealistic effect for a fluffy newborn lamb.

The triple outline that separates the lamb from the background consists of small amounts of medium gray-and-pink tweed, light gray, and very light gray.

You'll need some black-and-gray tweed for the lamb's head and legs.

Dove. Use a grayed peachy pink. For the halo outline, use soft rose and pale pink.

Ground. Select a variety of tans, beiges, soft light greens, and light browns. Simmer them together with uniodized salt to achieve a good effect. The wools will look drab, but they will come into their own after you have hooked the blue sky and bright border.

For the grasses, use sandy greens, which will blend

better than bright greens with the sandy ground beneath the animals.

Sky.   Find a pretty blue-and-white tweed if you can, and enhance it with a light overdye of Sky Blue. For a modified shadow background around the figures, overdye some of the blue wool in weak Olive Green. The subtle difference between the values will push the figures out from the sky.

Borders.   As shown in the color photo, the borders were hooked in dark green and red tweeds, as is. The outermost border is a medium brown tweed.

Hooking

Start with lion. Outline his face, ears, and head in rusty brown. Use the grayed brown for the shadows on his body. The tip of his tail repeats some of the lighter, brighter tones from the mane.

Hook the outline of the cub in dark orangy tan, and fill in with lighter tones.

For the lamb, start with a triple outline on the white parts: one row of medium gray-and-pink tweed on the outside, a row of lighter gray in the middle, and extremely light gray inside.

Hook the dove next.

Hook the grass in straight horizontal rows. Use slightly darker values close to the animals, especially the lion. To strengthen the outline around the fleecy white parts of the lamb, first hook a line of medium-dark taupy gray.

The sky is next. Again, hook in horizontal rows.

Complete the borders.

Finishing

Follow the directions for binding the edges given in the chapter Finishing Touches.

Mother Cat and Kittens

Worked in ¼-inch strips, this easy design can be completed in just over two weeks. Because it calls for tweeds and spot-dyed wools, and no shading, it is a good rug for the beginning hooker to try. But experienced hookers will want to do it, too: uncomplicated patterns such as this are a pleasant diversion.

Colors

Mother Cat. As pictured, the nursing mother was hooked in mottled grays and outlined in a darker gray. Her eyes are green.

Kittens. Select very dark gray tweeds for the one, and light and dark tweeds in tan and brown tones for the other.

Background. Overdye a gray and rose tweed in weak Rust dye.

Border. A bone tweed and a pale grayed-green tweed complement the colors of the cat and kittens. The outer border consists of greens that harmonize with the cat's eyes and, finally, darker rust tones of the background.

Hooking

Mother Cat and Kittens. Hook the kitten on the right first, then the one at left, and then the mother cat.

Mother cats—and other mammals—lick their newborns, not only to clean them, but also to stimulate their circulatory, digestive, and elimination systems. Anyone rearing an orphan kitten needs to provide as close an approximation of the mother's licking as possible. You can use a little cloth pad made of a rough-textured material like terry cloth, and dip it in warm water. The mother cat devotes fully fifty percent of her time to licking her babies; you can see how important this instinctive activity must be.

Mother Cat and Kittens

Background. Studying the photograph will help you see how the background was hooked. Start by hooking two rows all around the cat family. Then work two rows on the scalloped inside edge of the border. Fill in the small pools that form between your two sets of outlines.

Finally, hook the wavy border and the border background at the outer edge.

Finishing

Follow the directions for binding the edges given in the chapter Finishing Touches.

Welcome, Friends

Every home needs a cat waiting by the door to welcome our friends, and this sweet, homey little rug fulfills its mission beautifully.

Using muted tweeds and spot-dyed wools, without any bright colors, you can achieve a general effect of softness. You can also finish the rug quickly, since it calls for ¼-inch-wide strips.

Colors

Cat.   The cat's face uses six tweeds:

1   light browns
2   light golds
3   light grays
4   medium grays
5   dark grays
6   grayed peachy-pinks

For the body, use a dark gray tweed and a medium gray tweed. The legs are oatmeal.

Bushes.   Use spot-dyed green.

Ground.   Use spot-dyed tans.

Sky.   Use a soft gray-blue tweed.

Banner.   Use soft grayed orange and a dark blue tweed.

Welcome, Friends

The tweed I used was a thready type of wool. Although it can be a bother to cut and hook because it unravels so easily, the tightly wound threads will wear well.

Hearts.   Use rosy-red tweeds.

Border.   In the wavy arc, repeat the tweeds used for the cat's face.

For the zigzag line, use plain medium-brown wool.

For the outer edge of the rug, use a darker, richer medium-brown.

For the triangles, select four or five plain and

The six tweeds used for the cat's face are hooked as shown. **Color key:** 1) light browns; 2) light golds; 3) light grays; 4) medium grays; 5) dark grays; 6) grayed peachy-pinks.

tweedy dark reds and three or four brown tweeds. You'll also need a small amount of very rich, dark gold tweed.

Hooking

Cat.   First hook the cat's face, following the numbers in the diagram.

Hook the tail next. To make the tail more visible against the dark grays of the cat's body, use a medium-light gray tweed along its top edge.

Now do the two front legs and the rest of the body. Note that the outline changes from tan spot-dyed wool around the legs to medium gray around the paws. This helps separate the cat's paws from the ground.

Background.   Hook the ground area, bushes, and sky next.

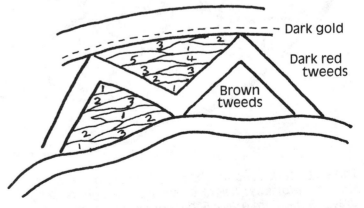

Use your three or four brown tweeds for the inside triangles. Hook them in narrow overlapping lines, as shown. Do the same with the four or five dark red tweeds in the outer triangles. A line of rich, dark gold (shown by the dotted line) separates the red triangles from the medium brown border.

Banner. Do the letters first and then the background behind them. Around the ends and lower edge, hook a single row of the tan spot-dyed wool from the ground.

Border. First, hook the two hearts and the wavy arc inside the triangles. Then, hook the zigzag border and triangles as indicated in the diagram.

Below the banner and around the circular edge of the rug, use the darker, richer medium brown wool. Separate it from the red triangles by a line of the rich, dark gold tweed.

Finishing

Strengthening the edges with cording is especially important for a rug that will receive heavy use just inside your front door. Follow the directions in the chapter Finishing Touches.

Tales abound of lost cats tracking down their human families. Cats have been known to travel hundreds of miles, taking many weeks or months to reach their goals. How they are able to find their way is a total mystery.

Joan Leith Mosheim

Dip dyeing produces wool with a subtle transition from light to dark, as in the red piece. Spot-dyed wool, like the olive green, creates a beautiful effect when hooked. The blue wools are an example of gradation dyeing.

"Kitten" chair pad, hooked in wool and cotton on burlap, nineteenth century. Courtesy of Stephen Score Antiques, Essex, Massachusetts.

A primitive rug, whether a genuine antique or a modern hooking in the primitive style, complements country furniture and collectibles. Photo by Jessie Walker. Reproduced by permission from Country Living (June 1986), © 1986 by the Hearst Corporation.

"Lion" pattern by Edward Sands Frost, burlap, unhooked, early 1870s. Frost used metal stencils to print his patterns, a different stencil for each color. The original stencils are now in the collection of the Henry Ford Museum in Dearborn, Michigan. Courtesy of Family Tree Antiques, Bridgton, Maine.

"Lion" pattern by Edward Sands Frost, hooked in wool and cotton on burlap, late 1800s. Courtesy of R. Jorgensen Antiques, Wells, Maine. Note how the different background changes the rug.

"Lion" pattern by Edward Sands Frost, hooked in wool and cotton on burlap. The rug maker added her own embellishment of a diamond border. Courtesy of Heller-Washam Antiques (formerly Milk Street Antiques), Portland, Maine.

"Primitive Lion." The simple treatment—one basic color accented with dark lines and small touches of red and white—works well for this fierce lion. Courtesy of Lynne Weaver Antiques, Wenham, Massachusetts.

"Cat and Kittens," hooked in wool and cotton on burlap, late 1800s. The scrolls in the corners indicate that this piece may have been a commercial pattern. Courtesy of Mr. and Mrs. Dale Butterworth, Cumberland Foreside, Maine.

"Two Cats with Floral Sprays," hooked in wool and cotton on burlap, late 1800s. The cats strike a prim pose beneath flowering branches in this simply drawn, well-balanced design. Courtesy of Joy Piscopo, F. O. Bailey Antiques, Portland, Maine.

"Leopard" pattern by Edward Sands Frost, hooked in wool on burlap, late 1800s. A rare example, this design was among Frost's earliest patterns. Courtesy of Heller Washam Antiques (formerly Milk Street Antiques), Portland, Maine.

"Happy Cat," hooked in wool and cotton on burlap, c. 1900. This cat bears a startling resemblance to a teapot. The background was hooked in simple horizontal and vertical lines. Courtesy of Elizabeth Enfield Antiques, Rockport, Massachusetts.

"The Cow Jumped Over the Moon," hooked in cotton on burlap, c. 1920s. "Hey diddle diddle, the cat and the fiddle" is thought to refer to Queen Elizabeth the First, who was known to enjoy dancing in her apartments to fiddle music. Courtesy of Mt. Vernon Antiques, Rockport, Massachusetts.

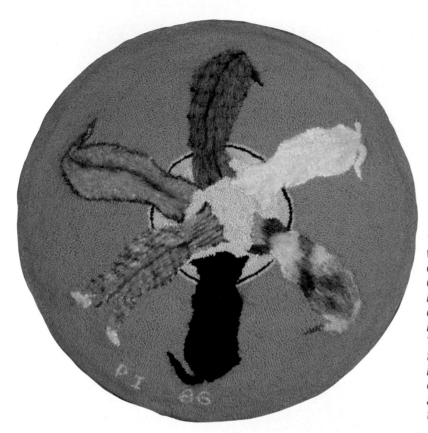

"Six Kittens," hooked in wool and handspun yarns of sheep, angora, and Old English Sheepdog on monk's cloth, original design by Peg Irish, Madbury, New Hampshire. These kittens are hungry: that so much feeling could be shown by the bend of an ear or the stretch of a back leg is testimony to Peg Irish's skill.

"Snack Attack," hooked in wool on burlap, original design by Joyce Long, Mechanicsburg, Pennsylvania. This battle-scarred cat, with his ragged ear, firmly grasps a goldfish. Joyce Long used the simple colors and hooking techniques of the primitive style.

"*Kibbles*" pattern by Joan Moshimer, hooked in wool on burlap by Karin Appel, Wilmette, Illinois. The out-of-proportion house and large stars surrounding the contented pet give this design its quaintness. To achieve the attractive unevenness of color in the background, Karin Appel crowded the wool into the dye bath.

"*Gerver Cat*" pattern by Lib Calloway, hooked in wool on burlap by Ramona Maddox, Chattanooga, Tennessee. Except for the terracotta background, pink nose, and green eyes, this rug was hooked entirely in black-and-white checks, plaids, and tweeds—fabrics that rug hookers sometimes pass up in the mistaken belief that they'll never find a use for them.

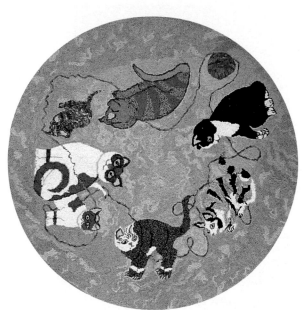

''Sally's Cats,'' hooked in wool on burlap, original design by Kim McGrew, Marietta, Ohio. The gray yarn unifies the lively pets in this design. The colors are closely related, and accented with black, white, and dark grays—an attractive color scheme with warm-toned wood floor or furniture.

''Deux Chats,'' hooked in wool on monk's cloth by Alice McElhose, Lincoln, Nebraska. The eight colors—gray-blue, black, white, dark green, rust, peach, and purple check—were hooked in the outline-and-fill method.

"Ann's Cat and Mouse," hooked in wool on burlap, original design by Ann Bornholdt, Bedford, New York. The pale gray outline is just the right depth both to blend with the fur and to set the cat apart from the busy braided-rug background.

"Cat Scan" design by Gretchen Whitman, hooked in wool on burlap by Dorothy Marosy, Sheffield, Massachusetts. Snug in a sunny window, this cat gazes out on the wintry landscape, no doubt recalling a summer mouse hunt in the barn. A tweed gives the gravel drive and spruce boughs their sparkle.

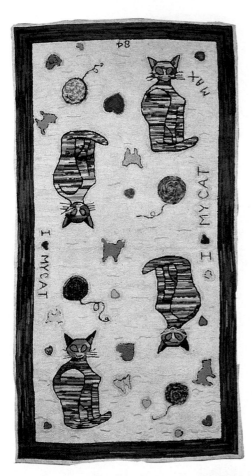

"*I Love My Cat*," hooked in wool on burlap, original design by Edith Martin, Islington, Ontario. The many colors, hooked horizontally, are effective and charming; this rug used up a lot of leftovers.

"*Bear*," hooked in wool on burlap, original design by Alice Osoff, Beverly, Massachusetts. This faithful rendition of the family cat dozing on his own hooked rug uses short lines of hooking in related bluish grays and grayed browns.

"Feline Fantasy" design by Don Waldera, hooked in wool by Virginia Waldera, Golden, Colorado. The ragged ear attests to this cat's feisty nature, but for now he is content to dream of mice. Soft brown-gray tweeds convey the feel of cat fur.

"City Cat and Country Cat," hooked in wool, original design by Joyce Fike, Medina, Ohio. The house and barn sit unexpectedly on the horizon, just as the cats sit on the road. This is a softly colored rug of attractive greens and blues.

"Four Kittens," designed and hooked by Joan Moshimer. Block designs, inspired by the quilting art, are favorites of rug hookers for the same reasons. They provide an attractive way to make use of a variety of checks, tweeds, and other wools left over from other hooking projects. Patterns made up of blocks can easily be enlarged to make floor rugs of any size.

"Tiger Cat," designed and hooked by Joan Moshimer. A pattern that is to be framed can often do without a hooked background.

"Lion and Lamb," designed and hooked by Joan Moshimer.
This peaceful primitive rug has no shading, making it a delight for
beginners.

"Mother Cat and Kittens," designed and hooked by Joan Moshimer.
A variety of dark and light tweeds are all that is needed to hook this
attractive rug. The three cats, with their different markings, contrast well against each other.

"Welcome, Friends," designed and hooked by Joan Moshimer. This half-round rug at the front door is a gracious way to welcome guests.

"Tabby Cat," designed and hooked by Joan Moshimer. This stunning tabby, with his glowing eyes, gives experienced rug hookers an opportunity to practice their shading skills. Hooking an equally detailed portrait of your own cat is easier if you have closeup photos to study.

"Staffordshire Cat," designed and hooked by Joan Moshimer. *"Fancy cats"* allow rug hookers to let their imaginations run wild. The color scheme may contain several values of one color or use wildly contrasting colors. This cat, with her jewelry and flowered shawl, looks out at the world with quiet complacency.

"Two Cats on a Pillow," designed and hooked by Joan Moshimer. There is a revived interest in silent companions, also referred to as dummy boards. They make unusual home furnishings that warm up the atmosphere of any room.

"Persian Blue," designed and hooked by Joan Moshimer. There's nothing like a beautiful model to inspire a beautiful rug.

"Hungry Lion," designed and hooked by Joan Moshimer. The king of beasts looks out over the savannah with a hearty appetite. The shadowy wildebeest in the background would make a delicious meal.

Intermediate and Advanced Projects

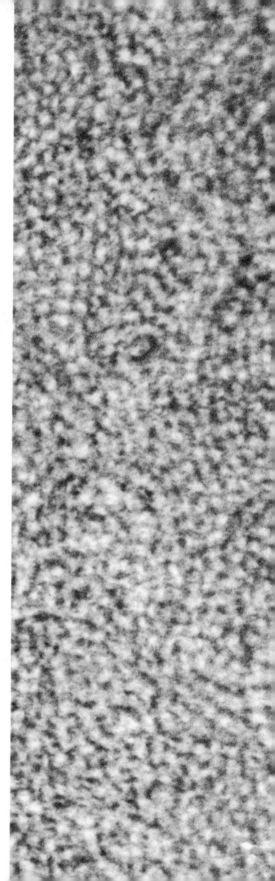

Tabby Cat

This kit was designed for rug hookers who have some experience in shading. Nevertheless, it requires only sixteen values of Potpourri Strippettes, which are convenient to use, since the swatches are already cut.

The kit, Tabby Cat MP 188, is available from W. Cushing & Company. It contains the pattern, wool strips, a color picture of the rug, and complete directions.

To achieve a realistic look, work from the numbered diagram and the color photograph. Used together, they will help you work out the colors and values.

Cut your strips 3/32-inch wide, or a #3 cut.

Colors

0	off-white	B	off-black
1	light taupe	C	pale green
2	medium taupe	D	light gold
3	gray-taupe	E	medium gold
4	medium brown	F	dark gold
5	dark brown	G	medium rose
6	darkest brown	H	dark rose
7	soft gold		

The background should be shades of burnt orange.

Hooking

Cat. Divide your task into sections as indicated and work on only one section at a time.

Tabby Cat

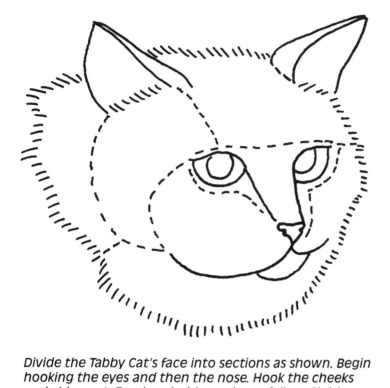

Divide the Tabby Cat's face into sections as shown. Begin hooking the eyes and then the nose. Hook the cheeks and chin next. Forehead, side, and ears follow. Finish with the back and neck ruffs.

For each section, study the color photo and note the location of the very lightest parts. Then find them on the numbered diagram; they're the 0s and 1s. Hook these lightest areas first.

Now return to the photo and find the very darkest areas. Find them on the diagram; they're the 6s and 5s and the off-black Bs. Hook these darkest areas second.

Finally, fill in the in-between values.

Working this way – observing carefully, then hooking the lightest and darkest areas, and doing the intermediate values last – you are making the project easy for yourself. You are demystifying the process. Once you've identified the lightest and darkest areas and hooked them, the shading begins to make sense. All that's left is to fill in the middle areas.

The wrong way to proceed is to work from light to intermediate to dark; most people run out of space before they ever get to the darkest values. It bears repeating: establish the lights, establish the darks, and only then do the intermediates.

You may find that you have to skip values because of a lack of space. Remember that in a cat's fur – and especially in a tiger cat's lovely silken coat – there are sudden shifts in color or value or both. Even if you can't always make a smooth gradation from light to dark, you will still achieve a natural look.

Background. The pale burnt oranges of the background highlight the browns and golds of the tabby cat. Fill in the background with neat, close loops.

Finishing

You might want to finish your hooking as a pillow, as in the photograph, but "Tabby Cat" also makes a stunning picture or wall-hanging. Steam-press, then frame your finished work.

Staffordshire Cat

Soft blues and greens, accented with gold, combine in this amusing "fancy cat" pillow. Or, let your imagination run wild and select other combinations you enjoy. Possibilities include yellows and burnt oranges, yellow-greens and blue-greens, or purples and reds.

Colors

W	white (1)
2	lightest blue
3	medium-light blue
4	medium blue
5	medium-dark blue
6	dark blue
8	medium green
9	light green
10	dark turquoise
11	light turquoise
12	dark gold
13	medium gold

You'll also need some gold or silver thread for the jewelry and a strip of 45- by 2-inch medium-dark wool for use in finishing the pillow.

Hooking

Study the color photograph and the diagrams as you work this project. You'll get a much better idea of how to hook the details if you compare the diagrams with the photo.

Staffordshire Cat

Start by hooking the cat's eyes. Outline the eyes and eyelashes with the same dark blue that fills the pupil. Hook a tiny dot of white in each pupil as a highlight.

Now hook the medium blue heart in the forehead. Outline it with a row of medium-dark blue and then a row of lightest blue.

The mouth and chin are dark blue with an outline of lightest blue. Use medium-light blue for the whiskers and nose. Finish the head by hooking the triangles of medium blue and dark blue around the head. Finish the head by filling in the white and doing the borders as shown in the diagram.

The bow and neckband are outlined with medium-dark blue. Fill them by alternately hooking a few loops of dark turquoise and then a few loops of medium green. This technique will blend the two colors handsomely.

The flowers, leaves, and scalloped shawl are hooked next, using the outline-and-fill method. All stems and leaf outlines are white. The background behind the shawl is dark blue and the scallops get gradually lighter.

The dotted lines indicate one row of 8. For the narrow outline around the cat's head and bow, hook one row of 5. To finish, hook two rows of 4 at the outside edge of the piece, then fill in the space between them and the narrow outline.

Hook the cat's jewelry next. For the bracelet on the left, use combinations of dark and medium gold to outline and fill the band. Then use white crisscrossed with gold and silver thread for the stone.

The bracelet on the right should be outlined with dark gold, as should the zigzag lines. Use the medium gold, along with the gold and silver thread, to fill.

Now hook the outline for the legs with dark blue. Inside that, hook a line of light blue, and then fill with white. Use medium-dark blue outlined with medium green for the tapered markings. Finally, finish off the front by hooking the background behind the markings with medium-light blue.

The borders, neckband, flowers, shawl, and tapered markings on the back are hooked just as they were on the front. The only differences are the back of the head and the tail.

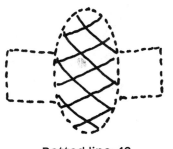

Dotted line: 12
Crisscross lines: 13

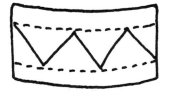

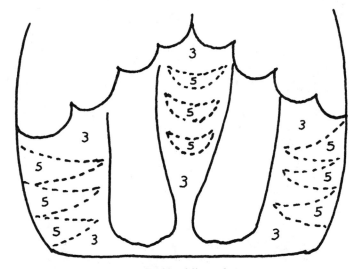

Dotted line: 8
Leg outline: 6

For the bracelets, outline with 12 on the dotted lines. Hook the crisscross lines with 13, then fill in the spaces with white wool and silver or gold thread. Outline the legs with 6. Inside that, hook a line of 2. Fill in the remaining space with white. The dotted lines indicate a row of 8.

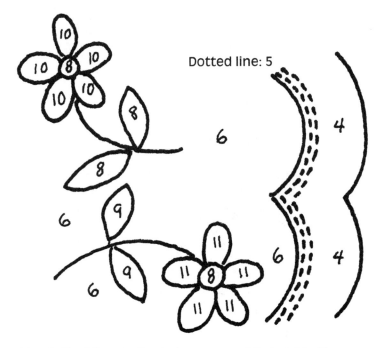

Dotted line: 5

The dotted lines indicate two rows of 5. Outside them, hook three or four rows of 4.

For the back of the head, outline the tapered markings with medium green and fill them with medium light blue. Everything else up to the borders is white.

Hook the tail last, following the diagram carefully. Each of the first five stripes is lighter than the one before. The sixth and subsequent stripes all have the same markings. Notice that where the tail lies on a light background, it's outlined with a dark color, and where it lies on a dark background, it has a light outline.

Finishing

Steam press the two hooked pieces. Approximately ⅜ inch beyond the last row of hooking, run a row of zigzag stitches or two rows of regular machine stitching. Trim off the excess backing just beyond the machine stitching.

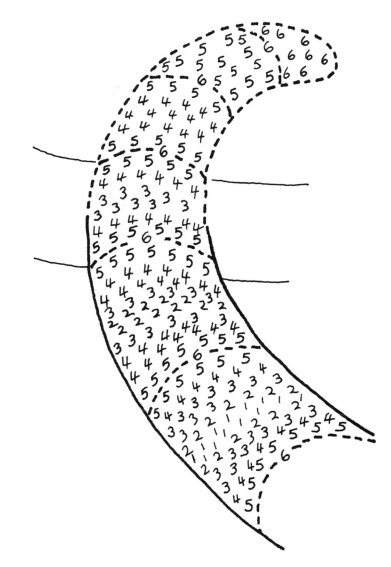

The tip of the tail is outlined in 6 (the dotted lines); the rest is outlined in 4 (solid lines). Separate the rings of the tail with 6 (the dotted lines). The rings at the base of the tail are hooked the same as the last one shown.

To join the two pieces, you need a strip of wool flannel in a harmonizing color. The wool strip should be long enough to go all around the pillow and as wide as you like (I used ⅝ inch). Turn the right sides of the hooked pieces together, and use the zipper foot on your sewing machine to sew them to the flannel so that no backing will show when the right sides are turned out. Don't sew the base together yet.

Now turn the pillow right side out and stuff firmly with fiberfill. Neatly stitch the hole up by hand.

Two Cats on a Pillow

These silent companions, or dummy boards, will stand on their own by the fireplace. If you cannot enjoy the loving companionship of a real cat because of allergies or apartment regulations, "Two Cats on a Pillow" will be the next best thing. They cost nothing to keep and feed, and you can even leave them behind with a clear conscience when you go on a vacation.

The wool was cut in ⅛-inch strips, or a #4 cut.

To mount a free-standing figure, refer to the instructions in "Finishing a Silent Companion."

Read through the directions first to understand where you are going. You may need to refer to Basic Dyeing to refresh your memory on dip-dyeing and spot-dyeing techniques.

Dyeing for the Cats

Sitting Cat.   Presoak a 15½- by 27-inch piece of off-white wool, then use the formula below for dip-dyeing. You will achieve the following colors:

white	medium rusts
cream	dark rusts
golds	dark rusty-browns
light goldy-rusts	brown-blacks

Dye Solutions
#1 = ⅛ t. Old Gold and
⅟₁₆ t. Mummy Brown in ¾ cup boiling water
#2 = ¼ t. Dark Brown and
⅛ t. Black in ¾ cup boiling water

D = dark
X = medium
L = light

Two Cats on a Pillow

Make a dye bath with 2 T. of #1 and add ¼ cup vinegar. Holding the presoaked wool by the narrow end, dip the piece so that the dark values cover the lower 10 inches or so, and the medium values extend about 10 inches above that. The remaining 7 inches of wool should range from very light to pale cream.

Add 1 T. of #2 and another ¼ cup vinegar. Dip the dark end of the wool to about 6 inches. Make sure the bottom 3 inches are a deep brown-black.

Set the wool, as described in Basic Dyeing. Cook it at 300° F. for about 45 minutes. Rinse it well and dry.

You may supplement the dyed piece with as-is wools from your treasury: brown and brown-black tweeds, lighter gold and rust tweeds. These will give your hooking some interesting textures.

Reclining Cat. Study the photograph. You will notice that the lightest values of this cat are somewhat darker than the lightest values of the sitting cat. And her darkest values are a bit lighter than the darkest values of the sitting cat. This difference in shading is a subtle way of visually separating the two cats.

For her darkest values, use some leftover browns from the sitting cat.

Presoak another 15½- by 27-inch piece of off-white wool and dip-dye it in a bath prepared from the solutions given below. You will achieve values in this range:

lights
medium lights
mediums
medium darks
darks

Dye Solutions
#1 = ⅛ t. Silver Gray and
⅛ t. Taupe in ½ cup boiling water
#2 = ½ t. Seal Brown in ½ cup boiling water

Make a dye bath using approximately 1 T. of #1 and add ¼ cup vinegar. Holding the wool by the narrow

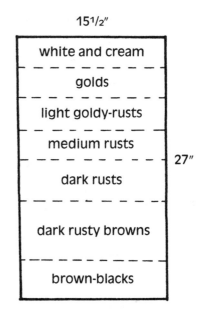

This swatch shows the proportions of the various dip-dyed values for the sitting cat.

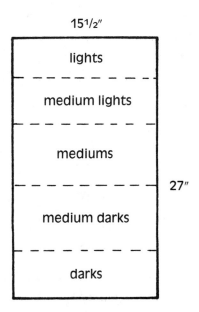

15½"

lights
medium lights
mediums
medium darks
darks

27"

This swatch shows the proportions of the dip-dyed values for the reclining cat.

end, dip the wool into the bath. The darkest values will cover nearly half the piece, the medium values the next 10 inches, and the medium-light and light values the rest of the wool.

To the dye bath, add 2 t. of #2 and another ¼ cup vinegar. Dip the bottom 4 inches of the dark end of the wool to achieve the deepest value of taupy gray.

Set the color. Rinse the wool well and dry it thoroughly.

Hooking the Cats

Take some time to study the diagram showing the flow of the cats' fur. This information will help you decide in which direction to hook the strips. To

It's important to follow the flow of fur to get a realistic look.

achieve the texture of real fur, hook in short, staggered lines.

The best way to fill in the erratic dark areas is to work with lines of different lengths, always following the flow of the fur. Change color and value often, and blend them together.

To hook a large area, establish guideposts for yourself. The darkest parts are easy to recognize; hook them first. Next, find and hook the lightest parts of the area. Once you have completed the darkest and lightest parts, the job will seem much easier: it is thrilling to see everything beginning to take shape.

Last, hook the intermediate parts, working from medium-dark through the succeeding lighter values.

Eyes.   Hook each cat's eyes before you do the rest of the head. You will undoubtedly have a selection of eye colors in your bag of leftovers. All you'll need is a strip or two of green or gold in medium and medium-dark values. Or dye off-white wool in Mint Green, Bronze, or Old Gold.

The thin black line around the eyes is best hooked with a dark thread pulled from a strip of wool. Pull the loops high, then trim them even with your other loops to keep the outline thin.

Note the tiny white highlights. Tuck these in last, using a fine hook.

Nose.   A medium value of dull rose is appropriate for both cats' noses. If you can't find any leftovers, use Old Rose dye on light gray wool.

Sitting Cat.   You should always hook figures in the foreground before those farther back. So the brown cat can be hooked entirely before you go on to the gray cat. Start with the face and head of the sitting cat. Put in the light values first, dark values next, and finally fill in the medium values.

A study of cats' faces reveals that many of these beautiful creatures have white or light areas surround-

You can see here how lines of hooking are staggered so that no sharp divisions occur and the values are blended.

Start with the sitting cat and hook in the order indicated by the letters. The reclining cat is hooked second because it is behind the foreground figure.

ing the eyes. These areas contribute greatly to the cat's expression, as do the dark M marks on the forehead and other streaks above and alongside the eyes.

Once you've finished the face and head of the brown cat, you can move on to complete it. Do the chest next, followed by the legs. The leg on the right is nearer, so hook it first.

Now hook the dark values of the tail, followed by the rear leg. Lastly, hook the bulk of the body, remembering to hook the dark areas first, followed by the light and middle values.

Reclining Cat. You've already hooked the eyes and nose, so now go on to finish the face and head. Remember to carefully hook the light areas above and below the eyes and the thin dark streaks extending outwards.

Now go on to finish the gray cat. Hook the leg on the right, then the leg on the left. Follow with the dark shades of her chest, finishing up with the medium values on her shoulder.

Dyeing and Hooking the Red Pillow

In a luxurious red velvet pillow – these are pampered cats – there are no light highlights, as there would be in a shiny material, like satin. So the lightest part of the pillow has to be a medium value leading into the richly shadowed areas. There are no sudden value changes in velvet.

The Front of the Pillow.   To hook the front in horizontal lines, you will need extra-long strips of wool.

Start with two pieces of off-white or pink wool, each 12 by 40 inches. Both pieces will be dyed the same. Review the techniques for dip dyeing and spot dyeing, as given in Basic Dyeing.

Dye Solutions
#1 = 1/2 t. Crimson in 2 cups boiling water
#2 = 1/2 t. Maroon in 2 cups boiling water
#3 = 1/8 t. Orange in 1 cup boiling water

Soak the wool for a few minutes in hot water to which you have added a little dishwashing liquid. Dye the pieces to a medium value using about 8 T. of dye solution #1 (Crimson) for each piece. Cook the wool with ¼ cup vinegar for 10 minutes and remove it.

To the dye bath, add 3 T. of #3 (Orange) and 3 T. vinegar. Holding one piece of wool by one of the long edges (you will need to gather it somewhat), dip the other long edge in the dye bath to a depth of about 3½ inches. Dip the wool as evenly as you can; a large rectangular or oval pan makes this easier.

To the dye bath, now add 2 T. of #2 (Maroon) and another 3 T. vinegar. Turn the wool over and, holding

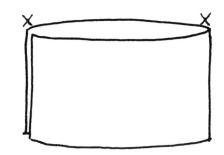

The dip-dyed pieces for the pillow should be folded as shown and held at the marked corners.

The purring of cats varies in volume and intensity. If you listen carefully and observe the purring of your cat, you will discover that different purrs have different meanings. A loud, rumbling purr expresses pleasure; a smooth purr may express boredom; and a high-pitched purr expresses pleasurable anticipation. I learned from my beloved friend, Purry Como, that a cat will even purr when he is sick or in pain, as if to reassure us that everything will be all right.

it by the edge you just dyed, again dip to a depth of 3½ inches.

Now add 10 T. of #1 (Crimson) and 3 T. vinegar to the dye bath. Turn the wool over and dip the first edge again until the wool will not absorb any more dye.

Save the dye solutions.

Set the color by immersing the wool very slowly into a pot of boiling water to which you have added ¼ cup salt and ½ cup vinegar. Do this gradually so that the water stays at the boil. Simmer for 30 minutes. Rinse the pieces well and dry. You will have wool that is a slightly orangy crimson at one edge, with deeper tones of crimson and maroon at the other.

To achieve a smooth gradation of velvety tones, you will work the strips in the order in which they are cut from the wool, so do not cut the wool until you are ready to hook the pillow.

Here's an easy way to keep the strips in order: cut only four at a time (on the #4 cutter blade) and immediately tape the ends of the strips, before they get mixed up. Take the strips off the tape as you need them, and cut the next four only when you're ready for more. That way, the hooked colors will flow as smoothly as they appear on the dyed pieces.

Hook the lightest values at the top of the front edge (beneath the cording), gradually shading into the deepest values at the bottom of the pillow.

The Left Side of the Pillow.   Take the leftover red wool and make it darker and duller by dip-dyeing it in a new dye bath made from small amounts of the leftover dye solutions.

Dye Solution
1 T. #1 (Crimson) and
1 T. #2 (Maroon) and
1 T. #3 (Orange) in 1 cup boiling water

To this solution add a very few grains of Jade Green to soften and dull the red slightly. Be careful; a few grains too many could spoil it.

Dye the red wool. Set the color as you did for the other pieces. Rinse and dry the wool.

Cut the strips the long way, keeping them in order by taping the ends until you're ready to hook them.

Hook the deeper values at the ends of the pillow and on the cording. Also hook the cording on the front, using four values – light at the top edge, shading quickly down to dark.

The Top of the Pillow.   Take the leftover red wool and spot-dye it with separate spoonfuls of #1 (Crimson), #2 (Maroon), and #3 (Orange).

In a large flat pan, sprinkle the wool with salt and cover it with water, and cook it at 300° F. for 45 minutes.

The Floor and Edges.   Use plain brown wool (Potpourri's Spice Brown value 4) for the floor around the pillow.

Hook three neat rows of a lighter brown (Spice Brown value 3) on all the edges: floor, pillow, and cats. Keep these loops neat and low, especially the outermost row. Soften the angles by rounding them as you go along.

Fill in the area between the two cats.

Finishing

Mount your cats as directed in the chapter Finishing a Silent Companion.

Hungry Lion

The king of beasts gazes over the plain. That hungry look in his eye – like the shadowy wildebeest behind him – suggests that he is starting to think about his next meal.

The detailed shading in the lion's coat is achieved with a large number of variously colored wools, some grayed, some in clear hues. Experienced hookers will enjoy the challenge, but the piece is not above the level of an intermediate, provided she has an enthusiastic teacher who can supply the necessary wools and encouragement – and provided she herself is enthusiastic, too.

Colors

The Lion. This lion is hooked in an impressionistic style, with many golds, browns, rusty golds, and sands. The more of these colors you have, the better. Look in your treasury of leftovers for some wools in clear tones and many more pieces in varying degrees of grayed tones.

For the eyes, nostrils, mouth, and jawline, you will also need small amounts of off-black, very dark brown, and white.

To supplement as-is wools, use the following formula as needed on light gray, medium gray, tan, beige, cream, light gold, yellow, peach, and light brown wools. Dip-dye to achieve gradations of tone.

Hungry Lion

Dye Solution
3 parts Golden Brown and
2 parts Brown Rust and
3 parts Old Gold

Overdye some pieces in weak solutions of Black to darken and dull your wools for shadowed areas.

The Background.   Look for tweeds in sandy-brown tones. At a rummage sale I found a 25-cent pair of ladies' tweed slacks that incorporated tan, off-white, rust, medium brown, and dark brown – colors that helped suggest the hot, dry African savannah. There was more than enough material.

The Wildebeest.   To convey the idea that the lion is dreaming of a wildebeest, I wanted soft, grayed, indistinct browns. There is no detail in the wildebeest. If you can't find the right wools as-is, select medium and light values of brown, rose, green, and gold, and dye them with onion skins (see Basic Dyeing).

To separate the wildebeest from the background yet keep him shadowy, you will need a small amount of the same dull pinkish gray that appears in the lion's mane.

Borders.   Review your collection of tweeds, especially men's sport coats, and look for dull greens ranging from dark to medium values.

For an accent between the border and the background, you might select some golds leftover from the lion and pieces of the onion-skin-dyed wool that were used in the wildebeest.

A hooked border enables you to display the finished piece on the wall or on the floor. If you plan to hang "Hungry Lion," you might prefer to use a wooden frame, in which case you don't need to hook a border. I would suggest painting the frame in soft dull golds and greens, then antiquing it.

Hooking

Study the black-and-white photo. The neutral grays will help you become aware of values rather than colors. Don't try to follow the color photo exactly, or be concerned if your lion doesn't turn out the same: your hooking should reflect you.

Observe the play of light values, medium values, and dark values. Note how much they help give shape and form to the varying levels of the face, nose, forehead, cheeks, and jaw. The black-and-white photo helps you separate in your mind the two important elements you are working with, value and color. We need to understand their separate functions and how to make them work together.

A color can have a light value (not much gray), or it can have a dark value (a lot of gray), or it can fall somewhere in the medium range. The full range shows easily in a black-and-white photo, since all the colors have been neutralized. Now you can distinguish the very grayed colors from those with little or no gray.

Note, too, that some of the grayed areas have very little color: the end of the nose just above the pink nostrils, for example, and also beneath the chin.

Cats communicate with their tails. When a dog wags its tail, we know it is friendly and happy, but when a cat wags or, more properly, **switches** *its tail, the cat is indicating annoyance. A hungry cat begging for food in the kitchen usually has its tail straight up; a male cat, advertising its top-cat status in the neighborhood, carries its tail bent forward over its head. Cats also use their tails for insulation. In cold weather, a cat wraps its tail closely around its curled-up body to conserve warmth.*

Eyes.   Hook the eyes first. Note the intense, slightly frowning expression of the lion as he scans the plain for prey. Much of this expression derives from the furrows in the brow, but try to get as much expression as you can in the eyes, too.

Whiskers.   These are usually white. Hook them before you fill in the area behind, and pull the loops very slightly higher than you will hook the surrounding loops. Don't try to crowd in too many whiskers.

Last, hook the spot at the base of each whisker, using wool that is not too dark: a grayish medium brown is about right. Cut the strips fine and tuck the loops in between the other loops, using a very fine hook.

This black-and-white photo shows clearly how the values change and blend in the lion's mane and face.

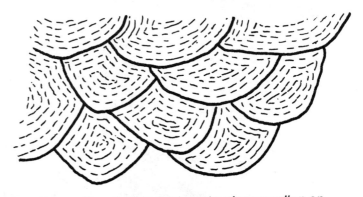

Use this scallop-shell technique to give your lion an attractive yet subtle background.

Nostrils and Mouth.   Very grayed pinks in medium to medium-dark values will look naturalistic. The white surrounding the nostrils and mouth should be not stark white but an off-white or eggshell.

A lion's mouth does not turn up in a smile. Give him a serious expression that matches the intensity of the eyes and the furrowed brow.

Background.   Use what I call my scallop-shell method to hook the background. The technique is extremely easy, and the allover effect is subtle and attractive. Follow the diagram.

The upper part of the background is hooked in vertical lines to suggest the tall grasses of the savannah. I used a tan and white tweed, interspersed here and there with short, 1½- to 3-inch-long vertical lines of a light, neutral tan.

After you have hooked the wildebeest but before you do the ground behind him, hook an outline of one row of dull pinkish gray.

Persian Blue

I made this 26-inch-square pillow for our four-year-old granddaughter. As I was hooking it, I had visions of the little girl stretched out on the floor, her elbows on the pillow, as she read her favorite books. Such are the dreams of a grandmother.

LC, as my granddaughter is called, knew that I was hooking the piece for her, but I was keeping the subject – a portrait of her long-haired blue cat – a secret. Imagine my delight when, as the cat's face was taking shape under my hook, she exclaimed, "That's Blue!"

The hooking is sized to fit a purchased pillow. The material for the back side of the pillow cover is a matching red nylon velvet (chosen because it is supposed to be long-wearing), with a zipper.

I started with a shaded pencil sketch of the face. This gave me a feel for what I would be doing later with my hook and shaded strips.

Dyeing

Dip-dyeing for the Cat. The best way to prepare wools for hooking long-haired cats is dip-dyeing. A piece of dip-dyed wool changes gradually from a deep tone at one end to medium tones and on up to light tones. If you then hook a strip with these changing colors and values, the shading will appear gradually, and the fur will automatically come out smooth and beautiful with no particular effort on your part. Remember that for most hookers a 16-inch strip will extend only about 4 inches when hooked.

Persian Blue

For "Persian Blue" the basic color I wanted was gray, with some blue tones and some taupes blended in. Dip-dyeing helps achieve this result.

You will need five pieces of off-white wool, each approximately 16 by 10 inches.

Dye Solutions
#1 = 1/2 t. Dark Gray in 1 cup boiling water
#2 = 1/2 t. Taupe in 1 cup boiling water
#3 = 1/8 t. Navy Blue in 1/2 cup boiling water

Make a dye bath using 3 T. of #1 (Dark Gray) and 2 T. of vinegar.

Holding the long end, dip a piece of 16- by 10-inch wool. You want medium-light values at the top shading down to medium dark. Be careful to allow enough room for the middle values. Repeat this process using three of the remaining pieces of wool.

Wearing rubber gloves, wring the wool as dry as you can and see whether the color is what you want. Remember that the wool will be lighter when it is dry. If the dye bath hasn't given you a dark enough value at the bottom end, add a bit more dye and redip. (It is better to add more dye than to have dyed the piece too dark.) Take care to dip a fair proportion of middle values. You don't want to run short of these values while you're hooking.

Lay all four pieces in a flat enamel or stainless steel pan.

To the dye bath, add 3 T. of #2 (Taupe).

Overdye one of the four Dark Gray pieces. Use this Taupe dye bath to darken the dark and middle values. Set the wool aside.

To the same dye bath, now add 1 T. of #3 (Navy Blue). Redip a second dyed piece. Use the Navy Blue to deepen the dark and middle values. Set the wool aside.

For the fifth 16- by 10-inch piece of off-white wool, prepare the following formula.

Cats' eyes have an iridescent, reflecting device behind the retina, causing the eye to reflect light in much the same way as a road sign reflects the lights of an oncoming car. Cats can see in dim light far better than we can. They can see best at dusk, which helps explain why they often ask to go out at that time of day. On the other hand, cats can't see as well as we can in bright sunshine.

Dye Solution
1 T. #1 (Dark Gray) and
2 T. #2 (Taupe) and
1 T. #3 (Navy Blue) in 1 cup boiling water

Make a dye bath using 4 T. of this solution and 1 T. of vinegar. Dip the fifth 16-by-10-inch piece to obtain medium-dark values at the bottom, medium values in the middle, and medium-light values at the top.

Set the color in all five pieces, and rinse and dry the wool.

Reserve the dye solutions.

Straight Dyeing for the Cat.   You will also need some light tones and some dark. These are not dip-dyed. Use two pieces of off-white wool, each 12 inches square.

For the light tone, dye one piece in a small pan with just a couple of inches of water, using the following formula.

Dye Solution
1/4 t. #2 (Taupe) and
1/4 t. #3 (Navy Blue) and
2 T. uniodized salt in enough boiling water to fill the pan to a depth of 2 inches

Simmer the wool in this weak dye bath for about 20 minutes. The resulting light tone will be very useful.

Rinse and dry the wool.

For the dark tone, dye the other 12-inch-square piece as you did the first, but use the following formula.

Dye Solution
2 T. #1 (Dark Gray) and
1 T. #2 (Taupe) and
3 T. #3 (Navy Blue) and
2 T. uniodized salt

Simmer the wool for 20 minutes. Set the color, and rinse and dry the wool.

Eyes.   Blue's deep orange eyes can be hooked in three values of bright rusty-gold. Look for as-is gold and yellow wools in your bag of leftovers, or dye small pieces of wool as follows.

Dye light rust and light yellow wool in Buttercup Yellow.

Or dye off-white wool in Buttercup Yellow to which you have added a few specks of Rust dye.

Background.   As pictured, the background for "Persian Blue" makes use of four red and rose wools, two plaids and two plain. I overdyed them in Buttercup

Yellow to brighten them up a bit and also to unify them. The result was a group of reds in varying depths of color, which allowed me to start at the top with the lightest values and work down to dark at the base.

To keep the reds separate in your work basket, you can bind them with strips of grocery-bag brown paper, held in place with tape. Identify each value with a number.

Hooking

Eyes. Start with the eyes. Outline them in a thin line of black.

Initially, I tried a very dark gray outline. When the shadows were hooked in, however, the gray was not strong enough to delineate the eyes, so I carefully pulled it out from the back side and tried again. Black gives better contrast.

Fur. The direction in which you hook the rows helps give the effect of a cat's fur. This cat engages us head-on; the area between the eyes is the place from which the directional lines start swinging out in graceful arcs.

Fan the lines of hooking so that darker or lighter values can be blended in. Notice that on the cheeks, short dark lines form a kind of rough outline. Then you can loosely work in the darker spots at the base of the whiskers. Finally, fill in the rest of the cheeks in medium-light values, following the direction of those short dark lines. By fanning them out, you can blend in other values.

Medium and light values (shown here as heavy and light lines) blend together in the cat's cheek. If necessary, cut your strips thinner to hook in tight places.

If a dip-dyed strip doesn't come up to the value you need to match or harmonize with the adjacent loops, just pull it up to the correct value and snip off what's in between. But don't throw the excess away. Keep such snippets in a small pile near at hand, for they will be just what you need later.

As you work with these varying values, you will develop a keen eye. Say you need a middle value to go between two areas that would otherwise jump too

As you begin to run out of one value for the back-ground, leave spaces in which to hook the next value. The colors will blend beautifully. Notice how I gather and number my batches of dyed wools.

abruptly from dark to light. If there is not enough space between them to make a smooth transition of several values, you must select the one in-between value that's right, the value that makes the small space count.

Background. I worked the background in straight rows. If you will run out of, say, value #1, blend it with value #2. Allow plenty of space to hook #2 around the rows of #1.

Notice that Blue's ruff ends in sharp points, and that the negative space between the tufts of fur also ends in points. It is essential to keep both kinds of points as sharp as possible. There is room for only one strip of background (or fur) at the points, so avoid packing the spaces and use thin strips.

To achieve a good sharp point, clip the end of the strip after you have hooked the last loop, then take it between thumb and forefinger and give it a slight twist. This point will be held in place by the surrounding loops. (Remember this trick for finishing the details on other hooked pieces, especially for leaf veins.)

Finishing

Wall hanging, pillow, or rug: your Persian will be a spectacular decorative accent in your home.

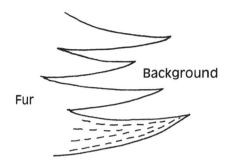

Fur is naturally tapering. Each of the four rows of hooking stops at a different place to preserve the point. Reverse this procedure when you hook the background, which forms its own points into the fur.

The Monetary Value of Hooked Rugs

After years of being virtually ignored by the general public, hooked rugs are beginning to be more widely appreciated. The lack of interest in hooked rugs in years past may have been unwittingly perpetuated by women themselves. The rugs were seen as "women's work," of no real value beyond the deep satisfaction that women received from the actual activity of hooking.

In today's social climate, women are more conscious of their potential in every field. Partly as a consequence of this changing attitude, hooked rugs are being viewed more realistically, as exquisite works of art in many cases, or at least as lively examples of the wit and imagination of their makers.

Cathy Comins of Art Underfoot Inc. is actively engaged in merchandising contemporary hooked rugs in the New York area. When she saw her first hooked rug at a craft show, she declared, "I was mesmerized by the direction and the rhythm in the movement of the pile . . . the beauty, charm and whimsy I saw being created was unlike anything I had ever seen . . . I was hooked!"

Cathy looks forward to the day when the American public is knowledgeable enough to recognize a genuine traditionally hooked rug – one that has been painstakingly made by hand with narrow strips of wool flannel. There are spiritless rugs, many imported from China, made with an automatic needle and yarns worked from the back side of the rug that are touted as genuine hooked rugs by some dealers. These rugs are as different from the real thing as a rowboat is from a cruise ship. There can be no comparison.

Among Cathy's customers are high-ranking politicians, cabinet members, and leading corporate executives. She believes that as hooked rugs become more visible and as the news media begin to notice the unique beauty of handmade rugs, then the public, too, will become more aware of them. Textiles as a whole have increased in popularity and value over the past few years. Prices have at least quadrupled.

When *HALI, The International Magazine of Fine Carpets and Textiles* was first published a number of years ago, it was a boon for all textiles. *HALI* mostly features Oriental rugs, but it also includes embroideries and other needleworks, tapestries, batiks, weavings, and more recently, hooked rugs. Hooked rugs will probably be included more often as more people become interested in making and collecting them and as people recognize their true value.

Rug hookers who would like to sell their rugs are becoming aware of the increased prices being paid for good hooked rugs. They wonder, "How much can I expect to get for my hookings?"

Answering that question is almost an art in itself; prices vary as much as the rugs do. We need to evaluate our work as if we were the buyer; as the seller, we are bound to be biased. We must rate the quality of the hooking, the quality of the color and design, and the quality of the finishing. We must ask ourselves some pertinent questions:

Is the rug an original design and the only one of that design?

It's more valuable if it is a single original.

Are the wools mill-dyed or custom hand-dyed?

Usually a rug made with wool that was hand-dyed and planned specifically for that rug is worth more.

Is the rug finished well? Does it have a strong, well-made edge with no tails left hanging on the reverse side and no small areas left unhooked? Has it been steam pressed?

It is the reflecting device behind the retina that causes cats' eyes to shine in the dark. In the not-so-distant past, the eerie glow of their eyes brought misery and degradation to the feline species; cats were assumed to be affiliated with devils, witches, and witchcraft.

Attention to these details will increase the value of the rug.

Does the rug have a strong foundation?

Linen is considered to be the backing that will last longest, but cotton and good-quality burlap are perfectly acceptable.

Are the design and colors pleasing and well balanced?

Whether a rug is "pleasing" is a highly subjective determination; it is best to get candid opinions from a number of people.

Does the background contribute to the harmony of the overall design?

In the best rugs, the background is a strong element of the appeal of the rug.

Does the rug "stand out from the crowd?" In other words, is it exciting?

Again, you may need to seek the opinions of others. An exciting rug will certainly command a higher price.

Lastly, what is the market like? For example, what is the financial status of the prospective buyer and what is the location of the sale?

A wealthy client may expect to pay more for a fine hooked rug than a person of more moderate means would. And in a large city or in a resort area, where prices in general are inflated, a rug will certainly command a better price than it would in a rural village.

In addition to considering the questions above, you will need to calculate how many hours you have worked on a rug and how much money you have invested in it. You should recognize that your investment in the rug is more than just the costs of the materials. There are also costs associated with working in your home: heating and cooling, electricity or gas for appliances, insurance, cleaning, and maintenance. It is common to double the cost of the materials to compensate for these hidden expenses.

Then you must decide how much you expect to be paid per hour. Many women grossly underpay themselves; astonishingly, some women pay themselves less than the minimum wage. They think that because they did the work at home or because they did it for pleasure, their time is not worth much. Wrong, wrong, wrong! Don't let your decision about how much to charge be influenced by personal factors. Instead, consider the beauty, decorative value, uniqueness, and yes, status of the article being offered for sale.

Once you have decided on an hourly rate, you must factor in one more cost – the commission that is paid to the gallery, craft store, or agent who sells the rug. You need to know what rate of commission the dealer will receive and whether the commission will be added to your asking price or taken from it.

The important thing is to arrive at a figure that is in harmony with the rug's true value, one that adequately compensates you for your special knowledge, for your skill and talent, and for the hours you have devoted to hooking the rug.

Sources of Supplies

APPLETON KRAFTS & SUPPLIES, 50 Appleton Ave., S. Hamilton, MA 01982. Complete line of rug-hooking supplies.

BRAID-AID, 466 Washington St., Pembroke, MA 02359. Complete line of supplies for hooked and braided rugs.

CARIJARTS, 2136 Silver Lane Dr., Indianapolis, IN 46203. Unique patterns for rug hooking.

W. CUSHING & COMPANY, P.O. Box 351, Kennebunkport, ME 04046. Manufacturers of Perfection Dyes.

DKS DESIGNS, P.O. Box 202, Mt. Calvary, WI 53057-0202. Complete line of traditional and primitive hooking patterns. Featuring the Australian Collection. Catalog available.

DESIGNS TO DREAM ON, Jane McGown Flynn, Inc., P.O. Box 1301, Sterling, MA 01564. Complete line of supplies for traditional and tapestry rug hooking. Catalog available.

DiFRANZA DESIGNS, 25 Bow St., North Reading, MA 01864. Patterns and kits for rugs. Complete line of rug-hooking supplies. Catalog available.

DORR MILL STORE, P.O. Box 88, Guild, NH 03754-0088. Wool by the yard. Catalog available.

EMMA LOU'S HOOKED RUGS, 8643 Hiawatha Rd., Kansas City, MO 64114. Primitive rug patterns printed on monk's cloth or burlap.

JEANNE FALLIER, The Rugging Room, P.O. Box 824, Westford, MA 01886.

FORESTHEART STUDIO, 21 South Carroll St., Frederick, MD 21701. Rug hooking, weaving, spinning, and other uncommon fiber arts. Supplies, equipment, instruction, and finished work.

HARRY FRASER CO., General Delivery, Stoneville, NC 27048. Fraser frames and a complete line of supplies for primitive rugs. Catalog available.

GINNY'S GEMS, 5167 Robinhood Dr., Willoughby, OH 44094. American Indian and Oriental patterns. Acid dyes and formula booklet. Catalog available.

HEIRLOOM CARE, INC., P.O. Box 2540, Westwood, MA 02090. Rug cleaner for the professional care of hooked rugs. Includes natural-fiber brush and complete instructions.

JACQUELINE DESIGNS, 237 Pine Point Rd., Scarborough, ME 04074. Complete line of supplies for hooked rugs. Catalog available.

MAYFLOWER TEXTILE COMPANY, P.O. Box 329, Franklin, MA 02038. Manufacturers of the Puritan Lap Frame.

MORTON HOUSE PRIMITIVES, 9860 Crestwood Terrace, Eden Prairie, MN 55347. Complete line of supplies for primitive rugs. Catalog available.

JOAN MOSHIMER (W. Cushing & Company), P.O. Box 351, North St., Kennebunkport, ME 04046. Cushing's Perfection Dyes, patterns, instruction, kits, and a complete line of supplies for traditional and primitive rugs, and a display of finished rugs.

NEW EARTH DESIGNS, Beaver Rd., RR 2, Box 301, LaGrangeville, NY 12540. Patterns silk-screened on burlap, rug warp, monk's cloth, and 100 percent linen. Catalog available.

JANE OLSON, P.O. Box 351, Hawthorne, CA 90250. Complete line of supplies for rug hooking and braiding. Catalog available.

PRO CHEMICAL & DYE, INC., P.O. Box 14, Somerset, MA 02726. Commercial dyes, pigments, and auxiliaries for the surface coloration of fiber. Catalog available.

RITTERMERE-HURST-FIELD, Box 487, 45 Tyler St., Aurora, Ontario CANADA L4G 3L6. Wools, patterns, and other supplies for hooked rugs. Catalog available.

RUG HOOKING Magazine, Cameron & Kelker Sts., P.O. Box 15760, Harrisburg, PA 17105. Bimonthly source of information on traditional hand-hooked rugs. Provides how-to's, historical profiles, dye formulas, and patterns. $19.95 for one year's subscription ($24.95 in Canada, $35 overseas).

RUTH ANN'S WOOL, R.D. #4, Box 340, Muncy, PA 17756. Wool in natural, white, and 28 colors.

SEA HOLLY HOOKED RUGS, Sea Holly Square, 1906 N. Bayview Dr., Kill Devil Hills, NC 27948. Hand-dyed wool by the yard or pound. Finished pieces and rug-hooking supplies also available.

SWEET BRIAR STUDIO, 866 Main St., Hope Valley, RI 02832. Patterns and supplies for traditional and primitive rugs. Catalog available.

THE TRIPLE OVER DYE FAMILY, 187 Jane Dr., Syracuse, NY 13219. How-to booklets with formulas for triple overdyeing.

YANKEE PEDDLER, 57 Saxonwood Rd., Fairfield, CT 06430. Patterns and other supplies for primitive and traditional rugs. Catalog available.

Glossary of Rug Hooking Terms

"AS IS": Wool, usually obtained from old clothing, that is suitable for use as it is, without being over-dyed.

BACKGROUND: The area behind the design in a hooked rug. In an outdoor pictorial, the background would be the sky.

BACKING: The fabric that forms the foundation of a hooked rug, through which the wool loops are pulled. The backing may be burlap, cotton, wool, linen, or a mixture of fibers.

BURLING IRON: Sharp-pointed tweezers used to pull loops out from the back of a hooked piece when necessary. Burling irons were developed by textile manufacturers for "burlers," workers who removed tufts of wool and other particles from wool cloth as it was being woven.

CONTOUR: The directions in which lines of hooking are made to help indicate shape. For example, a long, straight leaf is hooked in straight lines, and an apple is hooked in curving lines.

CUTTER: A hand-cranked machine used to cut wool into strips. The wool is guided through multiple cutter blades, which cut several narrow, even strips at a time.

FINGERING: A method of blending values from light to dark so that they effectively cover a given hooked area. Long and short lines of hooking, similar to the long-and-short stitch in embroidery, are used. The final effect is well illustrated by the interlocking fingers of two hands.

FRAME: The frame holds the rug pattern, which is printed on the backing, and keeps it taut, so that the rug hooker's hands are free to hold and pull the loops. Frames are available in a wide variety of styles and prices.

GEOMETRIC: A rug design that is characterized by the use of geometric shapes. The design is usually made up of repeated squares, rectangles, diamonds, circles, or ovals that are evenly spaced within a border or borders.

HALO BACKGROUND: (*Author's term*) The technique of hooking wool that is two or three values lighter than the background around all the design elements, creating a halo effect. A halo background is the opposite of a shadow background.

HIGHLIGHT: The lightest part of a flower, leaf, animal, or other object. Highlights are usually hooked with very light tints of the same color as the object, or with light tints of a related color.

HOMESPUN: Any fabric with a fairly open weave, similar to the weave of burlap, into which designs are hooked, leaving the background unhooked. The homespun may be dyed first in the desired background color. It is useful for making wall hangings, pictures, pillows, table mats, handbags, and articles of clothing—anything except rugs intended to be placed on the floor.

HOOK: A hook, similar to a crochet hook, set into a wooden or plastic handle. Hooks come in several sizes, from fine to very coarse, depending on the widths of the wool strips being used.

HOOKED RUGS: The hooked rugs referred to in this book are rugs made by hand with a crochet-type hook. They are hooked one loop at a time from the top side of the rug. The loops are made from strips of fabric cut from yard goods or from old clothing. Some "hooked" rugs are made automatically or semiautomatically of continuous yarn from the backside of the foundation fabric.

HOOKER: A person who hooks rugs and other articles by drawing up narrow strips of wool with a crochet-type hook through a foundation fabric to the top side of the work.

HOOKING: A general term for articles that have been hooked, such as floor rugs, wall hangings, pictures, table mats, coasters, decorative tiles, handbags, etc.

IMPRESSIONISTIC: (*Author's term*) A style of hooking that expresses the rug hooker's interpretation – or impression – of what is being hooked; it is not a realistic style. The impressionistic style is used particularly with florals, but it is not limited to them.

MESHING: The method of hooking wide loops that fit partially between the loops in the previous row, rather than lining up directly below them. Meshing helps make a close, luxurious texture, especially when wide strips are being used. (When narrow strips are used, there is less need for meshing.)

MOTIF: The dominant theme or design element of a hooked piece, seen against the background. The motif may be a geometric figure, a flower, a leaf, a scroll, an animal, a bird, etc.

OATMEAL: An off-white and light beige tweed, used "as is" by many hookers for backgrounds.

ORIENTAL: Hooked rug designs that are characteristic of Oriental rugs.

PADULA: An imaginary flower, not to be found in real life, on a hooked rug.

PATTERN: A design printed on a backing.

PRIMITIVE: A style of early rugs, made prior to the Civil War, that were often designed and hooked by poor housewives. The simple, sometimes very personal, designs were drawn from the heart and expressed the enthusiasm, wit, and talent of their makers. Many contemporary hookers enjoy hooking modern versions of the old primitives.

REALISTIC: A style of hooking in which every part of a design (for example, the petals in a rose) is carefully highlighted and shaded, using finely cut strips. Also known as *tapestry* hooking.

REDUCING GLASS: A lens that makes objects appear smaller – the opposite of a magnifying glass. It enables rug hookers to remain seated and still see how their work will appear from a distance.

RUG SHEARS: Shears made for the craft of rug hooking. They are used to neatly and easily clip off the ends of the wool strips even with the tops of the hooked loops. Rug shears are more convenient to use than ordinary scissors.

RUG TAPE: Woven cotton tape, usually 1¼ inches wide, used for binding the edges of hooked rugs. Lightweight wool, which has been cut on the bias, can be used to bind rugs, too, especially round or oval rugs.

RUG UNDERLAY: A pad placed beneath a hooked rug to prevent the rug from sliding and to absorb the wear and tear of walking on it.

SCROLL: A leaflike or fernlike ornamental design used to enhance and frame the dominant design, often used in Victorian rug patterns. It has evolved from ancient designs modeled after the acanthus leaf.

SHADOW: The darkest part of any object – a flower, a fruit, an animal, a bird, etc. – that is being hooked. Shadows are usually hooked with dark values.

SHADOW BACKGROUND: (*Author's term*) The technique of hooking wool that is two or three values darker than the background around all the design elements, creating the effect of a shadow. A shadow background is the opposite of a halo background.

SWATCH: A dyed piece of wool from which strips are cut to use in hooking a rug. A *gradation swatch* usually has five to eight pieces (each about 3 inches by 12 inches) with the first piece being fairly light and each of the other pieces being a slightly darker value of the same color. Other swatches consist of larger pieces of wool, either dip-dyed or spot-dyed, with a harmonious variety of colors on them.

TEXTURE: The structure and identifying quality of a finished rug. The texture of a rug depends on the evenness, or lack of evenness, of the loops; on the kinds of wool used to make the rug; and on the width of the strips of wool. Also, a rug hooked with a single kind of wool and a single width of strip will have a different texture from one hooked with a variety of wools and several strip widths.

VALUE: The relative lightness or darkness of a color. To an artist, value describes the amount of grayness in a color. Rug hookers also use the term to describe the strip that is one step lighter or darker than the strip they are using. A gradation swatch usually has five or more values.

Index

Notes

Notes

Notes

Notes